Kindly Light

May he support us all the day long,
till the shadows lengthen
and the evening comes
and the busy world is hushed
and the fever of life is over
and our work is done —
then in his mercy —
may he give us a safe lodging
and a holy rest
and peace at the last.

—John Henry Newman

Kindly Light

The Spiritual
Vision of
John Henry
Newman

Light

J. Murray Elwood

Ave Maria Press
Notre Dame, Indiana 46556

Acknowledgments:

Old Testament scripture texts used in this work are taken from the *Jerusalem Bible,* copyright © 1966 by Darton, Longman & Todd and Doubleday and Company. Used by permission of the publisher.

New Testament scripture texts used in this work are taken from the *New American Bible,* copyright © 1970 by the Confraternity of Christian Doctrine, Washington, D.C., and are used by permission of the copyright owner. All rights reserved.

International Standard Book Number: 0-87793-184-4 (Cloth)
0-87793-185-2 (Paperback)
Library of Congress Catalog Card Number: 79-52444

Front cover line drawing after a portrait by George Richardson.
Back cover photo of author: Firbolg Fotos, Ltd.
All inside photography by the author.

Printed and bound in the United States of America.

For David and Carol,
Bob and Cayt

Contents

Lead, kindly light, amid the encircling gloom,
  Lead Thou me on!
The night is dark, and I am far from home —
  Lead Thou me on!

Foreword

The lettering over the main entrance to the building I enter every day announces the Newman Center. His picture hangs in the front lobby and my ministry is sometimes described as the Newman apostolate. John Henry Newman. Victorian clergyman, Anglican scholar, Catholic cardinal. Authored the *Idea of a University,* preached a classic sermon, "The Second Spring," and didn't get on too well with the authorities in Rome. An interesting person, but about as remote, it once seemed, as Millard Fillmore or the Mexican-American War.

I can't describe when this book happened. Maybe it was the surprising response the Sunday I borrowed one of his sermons and preached it as my own; maybe I needed a role-model for a demanding ministry on a secular campus, or maybe it was those days in Oxford, sitting in the silence of St. Mary's, or visiting his rooms at Littlemore, touching the desk on which he wrote and kneeling where he once knelt to be received into the church.

Muriel Spark, the novelist, has noticed how somehow Newman seems alive; he is far less dead, she observes, than many of our contempories. I think I know the feeling. One is always surprised when reading Newman, not only by his rich crafting of words, or his brilliant understanding of problems that exist even today, but because he offers a quality of faith that remains as fresh as the springtime, as close to the heart of Christian belief as the Gospels.

Many people have helped me discover Newman. Meriol Trevor's wonderful two-volume biography details his amazing life with such delicate grace that it reads as easily as a bestselling novel. Pere Bouyer's study of Newman's spirituality and Father C. S. Dessain's research and writing helped place the events of Newman's times into their historical perspective.

I owe a special word of thanks to Sylvia Brownell, who first suggested the possibility of this book, helped resolve the difficult problems of style and polished the final product. I am also grateful to several other friends, A. Robert Casey, Edward J. O'Heron, Maryanne Schuessler, John T. McGraw and John J. Ziegler, because they indulged my Newman enthusiasms and always encouraged my literary efforts. Frank Cunningham, my editor, reassured some tentative beginnings and offered invaluable assistance. Carol Cary, with skill and generosity, deciphered the manuscript and typed the final copy.

The Newman Center
Oswego, New York
February 2, 1979

A Newman Chronology

1801 - Born, February 21, in London.

1808 - Attends Ealing school.

1816 - Family financial crisis and summer away at school; influenced by Rev. Walter Mayers "who was the human means of the beginnings of divine faith in me." Evangelical conversion.

1817 - 1820 - Matriculates at Trinity College, Oxford University.

1820 - B.A. degree

1822 - Elected fellow of Oriel College, Oxford.

1825 - Ordained priest in Church of England, May 29.

1828 - Death of his sister, Mary (January); becomes friend of Richard Hurrell Froude; named vicar of St. Mary's, the university church. Begins preaching regularly at St. Mary's.

1830 - Breaks with earlier Evangelical position; deprived of tutorship at Oriel.

1833 - Mediterranean journey; nearly dies of fever in Sicily (May). Composes "Lead Kindly Light" on way home, begins *Tracts for the Times* (September). The Oxford Movement.

1835 - 1836 - Builds mission church in Littlemore; death of mother.

1841 - *Tract 90* published—a Catholic interpretation of Thirty-nine Articles.

1843 - Resigns his parish of St. Mary's, Oxford; last Anglican sermon, "The Parting of Friends," preached in Littlemore church, September 25.

1843 - 1845 - Lives quietly in cottage at Littlemore as Anglican layman; begins writing *An Essay on the Development of Christian Doctrine.*

1845 - October 9, Father Dominic Barberi visits Littlemore, receives Newman into the Roman Catholic Church.

1846 - Leaves Littlemore, visits English Catholic centers, resides at Oscott College; at Wiseman's suggestion, travels to Italy (Sept.), enters Catholic seminary in Rome.

1847 - June 1, ordained Catholic priest; returns to England (December).

1848 - February 2, establishes oratory in England.

1849 - Pastoral ministry to poor in Birmingham.

1850 - Restoration of English hierarchy; Newman preaches "Christ Upon the Waters" at Bishop Ullathorne's installation, October 27.

1851 - Birmingham lectures on "The Present Position of Catholics" (June-September); Dr. Achilli sues for libel; Archbishop Cullen visits, invites Newman to Dublin (July).

1852 - Dublin lectures, "The Scope and Nature of University Education" (May/June); found guilty of libel (June); Newman preaches "The Second Spring," July 13, Oscott, England.

1852 - 1858 - Dublin, founds the Catholic University of Ireland; many travels between Ireland and England.

1854 - Formally installed as rector of Irish university; Archbishop Cullen blocks Newman's appointment as bishop.

1856 - Opens the University Church, Dublin; preaches to "lawyers and old ladies."

1858 - Returns to England; opens Birmingham Oratory school.

1862 - *Lincolnshire Express* erroneously reports Newman alive and well — in Paris!

1863 - Charles Kingsley attacks Newman in a book review for *Macmillan's Magazine* (December).

1864 - Newman replies to Kingsley's charge with his autobiography, *Apologia Pro Vita Sua;* Kingsley suffers nervous collapse.

1869 - 1870 - Vatican Council I; Newman takes moderate view of infallibility.

1875 - *Letter to the Duke of Norfolk* (January) on conscience and Catholic civil loyalties.

1879 - Made a cardinal by Pope Leo XIII (March); "the cloud is lifted from me forever."

1890 - August 11, dies at Birmingham Oratory; his epitaph: Out of the Shadows and Imagery Into Truth.

The village church at Littlemore where, in September of 1845, Newman preached his last Anglican sermon, "The Parting of Friends."

1.

Venture of Faith

On Monday, September 25, 1843, in a village church of St. Mary's, Littlemore, a few miles outside Oxford, an Anglican clergyman preached a sermon entitled, "The Parting of Friends." The altar of the small chapel was decorated with fuchsias and wildflowers; the pews were filled to overflowing with the minister's friends and university colleagues. ". . . Remember such a one in time to come, though you hear him not," the preacher concluded, "and pray for him that in all things he may know God's will, and at all times be ready to fulfill it."

When the sermon ended, most in the congregation were weeping; the clergyman left the pulpit, took off his clerical hood and laid it carefully across the altar rail. The gesture was unconscious, one he always made when receiving communion later in the liturgy. For his friends, however, the action had a special meaning; they knew they had heard John Henry Newman preach from an Anglican pulpit for the last time.

Newman's last sermon in this chapel at Littlemore, and his entry into the Catholic Church two years later, divide his life into almost equal parts. For the first half, from 1801 until 1845, he was a member of the Anglican Communion, and was enriched by the beauty and spiritual traditions of that faith community. Newman was one of the early leaders of the Oxford Movement which helped to renew and revive the Church of England in the last century; some of his greatest sermons and richest teaching come from this period of his life and Newman had an extraordinary influence, not only with Oxford undergraduates, but with many of the most brilliant minds of his generation.

As his Anglican years had been fruitful, so the Catholic half of Newman's life was marked with misunderstandings and failure. One Newman scholar, Father Stephen Dessain, has observed that during his Anglican days Newman was a conservative trying to revive and restore the Christian spirit when it was at a low ebb, but as a Roman Catholic he was a liberal attempting to correct wrong emphases and revitalize long-forgotten aspects of the same Christian faith.[1] Newman, as a Catholic, continued to grow in his understanding of Christian revelation and emphasized in his teaching his own unique insights into conscience as the voice of God, the developmental nature of religious belief and the role of an adult laity within the life of the church.

Many of his coreligionists, however, both in England and in Rome, were threatened by the depth and maturity of his vision. "He is the most dangerous man in all England," a papal chamberlain once wrote an English prelate about Newman's theology. Yet, when he died in 1890, Newman was a cardinal of the church and his epitaph read, *"Ex umbris et imaginibus in veritatem"*—Out of the Shadows and Imagery Into Truth.

His life spanned a century, 1801 to 1890. John Henry Newman was the eldest son of a middle-class English banker and a well-educated mother of French Huguenot extraction. He had three sisters and two brothers, and life in the Newman family, aside from a serious financial crisis after the Napoleonic wars, was full of laughter and love. Young John was intellectually precocious: he translated the Latin of Ovid and Virgil when he was nine, learned to play the violin at about the same age, and was reading the New Testament in Greek by the time he was 12.

The family belonged to the Church of England. This meant, as Newman later revealed, bible reading, pious sentiments, high moral standards and a vague sense of the providence of God. By the age of 14, John had decided "to be virtuous, but not religious." He enjoyed reading Thomas Paine's attacks on the Old Testament, Hume's *Essays Against Miracles* and had even copied out some verses of Voltaire which denied the immortality of the soul, saying to himself, "how dreadful, but how plausible!"[2]

In fact, Newman has related how religion made very little sense to him at the time. He was drifting towards skepticism when an event occurred that changed his whole future life. Because of the family's financial difficulties, John was left at boarding school for the summer vacation of 1816. He was befriended by an Evangelical minister, the Reverend Walter Mayers. Mayers was more pious than brilliant, but he impressed Newman by the obvious sincerity of his personal interest and pulpit oratory.

Newman was encouraged by Mayers to begin a

serious study of Christianity. As a result, his interest in religion, which he had previously rejected, was revived. His intellectual quest was accompanied by a hunger for personal holiness and an almost mystical awareness of the presence of God in his life. The intuition that overtook him that summer of 1816 was not just adolescent enthusiasm or an emotional experience, but a profound change of heart which overwhelmed him "in the thought of two and two only absolute and luminously self-evident beings, myself and my Creator."[3]

Newman went up to Trinity College at Oxford in June of 1817, was elected an Oriel Fellow in 1822 and ordained a clergyman in the Church of England in 1825. "I have the responsibility of souls on me to the day of my death," he wrote later in his diary, but regarded university teaching as the real field of his ministry.

Two Oxford associates influenced his theological growth about this time. Edward Hawkins, later to be provost of the university, offered some well-deserved criticism on the style of Newman's early sermons, especially his habit of arbitrarily dividing people into the saved and unsaved. "Men are not saints or sinners," Hawkins reminded him, "they are not as good as they should be and better than they might be." Newman's early ministry in a working-class parish also helped open his eyes to the unrealism and capricious nature of certain other Evangelical formulas.

Richard Hurrell Froude, elected an Oriel Fellow several years after Newman, soon became one of his closest friends and another influence on his way to theological maturity. Froude was a medievalist; he had a sense of the church as a historical fact, which Newman was yet to acquire. Through Froude, Newman came to an understanding of the real presence of Christ in the Eucharist, an appreciation of the sacramental system and an awareness of the role of Mary, the mother of Jesus.

In 1828, Newman was appointed vicar of St. Mary-the-Virgin, the Oxford University church. The main body of St. Mary's on High Street in Oxford dates from before the English Reformation and over the south entrance stands a battered statue of the Virgin and Child. After becoming vicar, he started daily matins, evensong and an early Sunday communion service. Newman himself preached at the afternoon service, Sundays and Feast Days, for 15 years. At first, the congregation consisted of only a few charwomen, college servants and storekeepers. Soon, however, undergraduates and even faculty began crowding into St. Mary's for Sunday evensong. One contemporary observes: "There was scarcely a man of note in the University, young or old, who did not, during the last two or three years of Newman's incumbency, habitually attend the service and listen to the sermons."[4] In fact, so attractive was Newman's preaching that one dean, envious of his influence, even changed the Sunday dinner hour to discourage the undergraduates; students then went without supper to hear the vicar of St. Mary's.

During the years he was preaching from the pulpit of St. Mary's, Newman was engaged in an intense study of the early church fathers. His *Parochial and Plain Sermons* thus reflects, not only his personal understanding of the spiritual life, but mirrors the primary sources, after scripture, of all Christian spirituality. Surprisingly, Newman's sermons, following the pulpit style of the day, were read rather than really preached. His gestures, vocal inflections and use of rhetorical devices, according to many contemporary accounts, were minimal, but he would usually pause slightly before reading significant passages. He always preached on a biblical theme based on one of the scriptural lessons for the day's liturgy, and his sermons, short for the age, would usually last 15 minutes or less.

In 1833, the English Parliament began an earnest effort to trim costs and correct abuses in its governmental institutions. The Church of England was included in this political reform by an *Irish Church Act* which rearranged the boundaries of several Anglican dioceses in Ireland and suppressed 10 bishoprics. Some high churchmen and Oxford clerics, including Newman, reacted negatively to this Parliamentary action. The real issue, they felt, was not a more efficient administration of the Irish dioceses, but whether the Church of England was a branch of government, or a divine institution deriving its authority from apostolic times.

On July 4, 1833, at a service in St. Mary's marking the opening of the Law Courts, John Keble protested the governmental move in a sermon titled, "National Apostasy." Newman always dated the beginnings of the Oxford Movement from the day of Keble's sermon.

Meetings of concerned clergy quickly followed and plans were laid to collect signatures for a petition addressed to the Archbishop of Canterbury. Newman, who had a lifelong distrust of committees, chose a different course of action. He began publication of a series of pamphlets, *Tracts for the Times,* from which the Tractarian Movement took its name. The first few tracts, addressed to the Anglican clergy, insisted that the church was of divine origin, upheld belief in apostolic succession and criticized proposed alterations in the *Prayer Book.*

As the Oxford Movement gained momentum, Newman began a serious study of the church of the early centuries. His purpose, at first, was to find in history support for the Church of England against the encroachments by the state. By 1839, however, he was trying to develop a theological basis for the Anglican position—between what he perceived as the errors of Rome, on the one hand, and the extremes of Protestantism, on the other. For Newman was aware that some members of the Oxford Movement were drifting towards Rome and he hoped, by his "Via Media" theory, to make it possible for them to remain in the Church of England.

Then there came the moment, in the course of his studies, when Newman was suddenly struck by a historical similarity. It occurred to him that an obscure fifth-century sect, the Monophysites, had cut themselves off from Rome, the historical center of Christianity, in much the same way that the Church of England was separated from Rome in the 19th century. "My stronghold was Antiquity," Newman wrote. "Now here, in the middle of the fifth century, I found, as it seemed to me, Christendom of the sixteenth and the nineteenth centuries reflected. I saw my face in that mirror and I was a Monophysite."[5]

Was the face in the mirror a grace or an illusion? Newman always believed that fidelity to conscience was a sure pathway to God, so he spent Lent of 1840 in the village mission of Littlemore visiting the sick, teaching catechism to the children and undertaking a period of prayer and fasting to discern the will of God. But his doubts persisted. "I am far *more* certain that England is in schism," he wrote to John Keble, "than that the Roman additions to the primitive creed may not be development arising out of a keen and vivid realization of the New Testament revelation."[6]

In 1841, Newman authored *Tract 90,* the last of his theological position papers. *Tract 90* was a Catholic interpretation of the Thirty-Nine Articles of the Anglican Creed, an attempt to preserve a tie between Canterbury and Rome. Its publication was greeted with a storm of protest; the Church of England of that day, as a whole, regarded itself more Protestant than Catholic.

With the publication of *Tract 90,* Newman had reached the "deathbed," as he described it, of his Anglican days; his sermon, "The Parting of Friends," that September of 1843 was his last gesture of love to his friends in the Church of England and to the faith community he held so dear. He resigned as vicar of his beloved St. Mary's at Oxford, and remained in seclusion for two more years at Littlemore as an Anglican layman. He continued fasting, began writing *An Essay on the Development of Christian Doctrine* and faced the unknown. To Edward Coleridge he wrote in November of 1844:

> What possible reason of mere "preference" can I have for the Roman Church above our own? I hardly ever, even abroad, was at any of their services. I was scarcely ever, even for an hour, in the same room with a Roman Catholic in my life. I have had no correspondence with anyone. . . . My habits, taste, feelings are as different as can well be conceived from theirs. . . .[7]

To John Keble, a few days later, Newman would add this fear about his future as a Catholic, "I am setting my face absolutely towards the wilderness. . . ."[8]

The personal cost of his final step was enormous, as he confides to his sister, Jemina, in March of 1845:

> At my time of life men love ease. I love ease myself. I am giving up a maintenance involving no duties, and adequate to all my wants. What in the world am I doing this for (I ask *myself* this), except that I think I am called to do so? I am making a large income by my sermons. I am, to say the very least, risking this; the chance is that my sermons will have no further sale at all, I have a good name with many; I am deliberately sacrificing it. I have a bad name with more; I am fulfilling all their worst wishes, and giving them their most coveted triumph. I am distressing all I love, unsettling all I have instructed or aided. I am going to those whom I do not know, and of whom I expect very little. I am making myself an outcast, and that at my age. . . . Continually do I pray that He would discover to me if I am under a delusion: What can I do more? What hope have I but in Him? To Whom should I go? Who can do me any good? Who can speak a word of comfort but He? . . . May He tell me, may I listen to Him, if his will is other than I think it to be.[9]

On a rainy night in the early fall of that same year, Father Dominic Barberi arrived at the cottage in Littlemore. The next day, October 9, 1845, Newman knelt on the stone floor beside his writing desk and was received into the Catholic Church. His Anglican life had ended; a new segment of his pilgrimage had begun.

Many reasons might be offered to explain the continuing interest in the life and writings of John Henry

Newman. That he was an intellectual genius, there can be no question; his theological views and educational theories are as exciting today as when they were first proposed over a hundred years ago. He was a man with an enormous capacity for friendship; the people he knew, the lives he touched and the incredible events of his own busy life could provide material for a dozen novels. Newman was a master of the English language; whether writing sermons, poetry, letters, novels, hymns or theology, the quality of his literary style is matched by few. He has also become a bond, in an ecumenical age, helping to reunite those two communions, Anglican and Roman Catholic, whom he so loved and to whom he once so faithfully ministered.

Newman's spiritual journey, his single-minded fidelity to that "Kindly Light" which first called him out into the wilderness and then continued to lead him on, is the value in his life which most endears him to contemporary Christians. God is best honored, Newman always believed, not only by external rites and worship, but by absolute obedience to his call from within. Newman's life is thus not only the narrative of a great intellectual quest for truth, but the story of a soul who struggled, his whole life long, to be faithful to that light of Truth which gradually revealed itself within his heart.

The chapters that follow offer some of the insights of Newman's own spirituality. Their source, for the most part, is those sermons he once preached at Oxford, from the pulpit of St. Mary's. These homilies found their inspiration in scripture, were directed to ordinary Christians living in the world and usually centered upon one or another of the major themes of Newman's spiritual teaching—conscience as the call of God, a personal love of Christ, the power of personal influence, the hiddenness of Christ, the pursuit of holiness. Newman's own holiness radiates from every page he ever wrote; nowhere, however, does his spirituality find a richer expression than in the sermons he preached at St. Mary's.

In a corner of Newman's beloved church, there is a Latin inscription carved in stone. The tablet was placed there by the English Franciscans and describes how, some 700 years earlier, the great theologian, John Duns Scotus, had once preached from that very spot on the theme, "The Lord Is My Light." Many centuries later, another Oxford scholar and convert, Gerard Manley Hopkins, would recall that day with a poem, *Duns Scotus's Oxford*. His words could apply equally well to John Henry Newman and his days at Oxford as vicar of St. Mary's:

> . . . this air I gather and I release
> He lived on, these weeds and waters, these walls
>   are what
> He haunted who of all men most sways my spirits
>   to peace.[10]

The pulpit of St. Mary's, The University Church, Oxford. Newman preached from this pulpit almost every Sunday from 1828 until 1843.

2.

Emotion, and Faith

Meriol Trevor, in her book, *The Pillar of the Cloud,* has described the stormy beginnings of the relationship between Newman and a headstrong young governess, Miss Mary Holmes. Miss Holmes was employed by an English family, but felt frustrated in the pursuit of her real interests, music and art. She wrote long, impassioned letters to prominent literary figures of her day, among them William Thackeray and Anthony Trollope. In 1840, Miss Holmes sent her first letter to Newman asking for his advice and signing herself "XYZ."

Two years and many letters later, Miss Holmes was passing through Oxford and stopped off to pay Newman a personal visit. Their first meeting was a disaster. The governess had apparently expected Newman to be an older man, a sort of father figure and spiritual oracle. She did not hesitate to tell him of her disappointment in his appearance and manner. Newman wrote her later, "As for myself, you are not the first person who has been disappointed in me. Romantic people always will be. I am, in all my ways of going on, a very ordinary person . . . I cannot speak words of wisdom; to some it comes naturally."[1]

Mary Holmes, with her romantic illusions about Newman, is a good illustration of those people who bring to a relationship with a counselor, spiritual director or marriage partner impossible dreams and unrealistic expectations. Some men and women will always seek a more enriching experience than they have a right to expect from another person, or group of persons. When their unrealistic expectations are not satisfied, then people like Miss Holmes always feel let down and disappointed; they blame others for not making their impossible dreams come true. No friendship, however loving, can take away all of life's loneliness; no group, however enriching, can fulfill all one's emotional needs; no liturgy, however creative, can satisfy all spiritual hungers.

Newman knew that what was true of social groups and human relationships was even more valid for the life of the spirit and a person's relationship with Christ. We should hope for great things from the Lord, he believed, but our spiritual expectations should be no less realistic than our earthly ones.

Newman observed how in Jesus' own lifetime, even though our Lord had accomplished "works which no other man ever did," the scribes and the Pharisees still persisted in expecting him to perform some decisive sign which would conclusively prove his words. "Teacher, we want to see you work some signs" (Mt 12:38). In answering their request, Jesus both denied and yet promised such a sign. He said, "An evil and unfaithful age is eager for a sign! No sign will be given it but that of the prophet Jonah" (Mt 12:39). He implied by these words that, while he would not conform to their expectations, some sort of sign, some miracle would happen.

On another occasion, the Pharisees were joined by the Sadducees, but their mission was the same: ". . . as a test [they] asked him to show them some sign in the sky" (Mt 16: 1). Joshua had once stopped the sun and the moon "in the sight of Israel." Samuel had caused thunder at harvesttime, so Jesus, too, was asked for a sign from heaven. He answered by promising them, not the kind they were expecting, but a sign from earth. This is why Jesus adds, "I assure you, no such sign will be given. . ." (Mk 8: 12). His sign was to be the sign of Jonah who was in the belly of the whale three days and three nights.

Earlier in our Lord's ministry, Newman also noted, the same unrealistic expectations had been expressed by another group, "What sign can you show us authorizing you to do these things?" (Jn 2: 18). Jesus answered in the same way, but with a different metaphor, "Destroy this temple, and in three days I will raise it up" (Jn 2: 19). He spoke, of course, about the resurrection, but they failed to understand his words.

What is remarkable in all these passages is that our Lord promised to effect a sign as great as those that had been worked by the Jewish prophets of old. But instead of working that sign in public, as people expected, Jesus' deed would be an event like Jonah's, a secret sign. Few would actually witness it, but it would be made available to all in faith. Later on, Thomas would refuse to believe in that sign, the resurrection, without seeing the risen Christ, but our Lord would praise those who believed without seeing and would imply that this would be the way for most of his followers.

When our Lord promises all Christians that he will be present in their lives, it is only natural, Newman explains, to expect that his presence will be felt sensibly.

> He who obeys the commandments he has from me
>> is the man who loves me;
> and he who loves me will be loved by my Father.
> I too will love him
>> and reveal myself to him (Jn 14: 21).

God's gracious presence within the human heart brings light, love and peace. These gifts, since they do not come of themselves, imply a Presence who is their source, a voice of whom they are the echo. But just as Miss Holmes once expected that Newman would be much more paternal, much more directive in their relationship, so there are Christians who want that inward manifestation of Christ to be more explicit than an echo, more sensible than a silent presence. These Christians approach their spiritual lives, Newman says, as if it were not more blessed to believe than to see:

> They will not be contented without some sensible sign and direct evidence that God loves them; some assurance, in which faith has no part, that God has chosen them . . . not considering that whatever be the manifestation promised to Christians by Our Lord, it is not likely to be more sensible and more intelligible than the great sign of His own Resurrection. Yet even that, like the miracle wrought upon Jonah, was in secret, and they who believed without seeing it were more blessed than those who saw.[2]

Our contemporary religious climate, for many social and historical reasons, is marked by a great variety of spiritualities and paths of prayer—bible fellowships, Marriage Encounter, teen seminars, prayer groups, healing services, discernment workshops. Feeling comfortable with a personal faith expression, in the midst of such a diversity of movements and ministries, is no easy task. Some Catholics are concerned because their traditional forms of piety now seem out of date. Others feel a vague sense of guilt; for while they really love the Lord, they are not able to experience that love with intense emotion of some other Christians.

Newman was very careful to point out in his preaching and spiritual direction that there were many times, in the course of salvation history, when the Lord was present to holy people, but they did not feel it sensibly; they became aware of the Lord's presence only after he had departed. Thus Jacob, after his vision, cries out: "Truly, Yahweh is in this place and I never knew it!' (Gen 28: 16). Manoah understood only after the angel had departed and said to his wife, "We are certain to die because we have seen God" (Jgs 13: 22). Gideon, too, did not sense God's presence at the time of his visitation, but became aware only later: "Then Gideon knew this was the Angel of Yahweh, and he said, 'Alas, my Lord Yahweh! I have seen the Angel of Yahweh face to face!' " (Jgs 6:22). Even Peter, while being freed from prison, had "no clear realization that this was taking place through the angel's help. The whole thing seemed to him a mirage." Only later, after he had escaped from prison, "Peter . . . recovered his senses . . . and said, 'Now I know for certain that the Lord has sent his angel to receive me' " (Acts 12, 9-11).

Many Christians, who have never had a direct experience of God's presence, become aware he has touched their lives the way Jacob and Gideon and

Peter became aware, only later and after the moment
of his visitation. These men and women can look back
upon the story of their lives and discern a certain pattern
of incidents and events. Why one path taken, rather
than another? Why did my life unfold in this way and
not in a different direction? Why this person and that
place, this event, a certain profoundly transforming
experience? The answer is God's loving care, his silent
presence in our lives. Like Jacob, many men and women
can say of their lives, "Truly, the Lord was in this
place, and I never knew it!"

Newman did not, therefore, feel it necessary for
all Christians to experience God's presence sensibly:

> Let no one think it strange to say that God
> may be holding Communion with us without
> our knowing it. Do not all good thoughts
> come from Him? Yet are we sensible that
> they so come? Can we tell how they come?
> We commonly speak of being influenced by
> God's grace and resisting his grace; this im-
> plies a certain awful intercourse between the
> soul and God; yet who will say that he can
> tell in particular instances when God moves
> him, and when he is responding this way or
> that? It is one thing, then, to receive im-
> pressions, another to reflect upon them and
> be conscious of them. God may manifest
> Himself to us, and that to the increase of our
> comfort, and yet we do not realize that He
> does so.[3]

There are some people, however, who do feel God's
presence in their lives and do have sensible religious
experiences—the gift of tears, baptism of the spirit,
overwhelming transports of joy. Some holy men and
women, like Philip Neri, Teresa of Avila and John

XXIII, radiated such a sense of peace and love that people felt good just meeting them. Other saints, for example, Alphonsus Liguori or Margaret of Cortona, felt so sorry for their past lives that they actually wept for their sins. So there are Catholics today who feel great joy in having found Jesus, or are able to shed sincere tears of repentance for their failures in the past.

Newman saw these sensible consolations of the Spirit not as a spiritual "basic," but as a help by which some Christians might be brought to more deeply religious lives. These graces, he felt, were offered to some souls by a gracious Lord, but were not necessary for all Christians. In fact, Newman was very cautious about encouraging excessive emotion in religion because he had observed, among the Evangelicals of his day, how for some people feelings can all too easily become an end in themselves:

> They think that to be thus agitated is to be religious; they indulge themselves in these warm feelings for their own sake, resting in them, as if they were then engaged in a religious exercise, and boasting of them as if they were an evidence of their own exalted spiritual state; not *using them* (the one only thing they ought to do), using them as an incitement to *deeds* of love, mercy, truth, meekness, holiness.[4]

Why do some Christians experience great consoling graces from the Lord after their conversion? Because without these gifts they might otherwise find the first few weeks and months of their new life very difficult. It is no easy task to overcome the patterns and habits of a lifetime. So the intense feelings new Christians sometimes experience are intended to serve as an inducement, an incentive, towards deeds: prayer, self-denial and loving service to others.

This is why Jesus, in one of the Gospel accounts of his cure of the Gerasene demoniac, would not permit the man to indulge his enthusiasm by joining the disciples. The man begged to follow Christ, but the Lord diverted the current of his newly awakened feelings into another direction: "Go back home and recount all that God has done for you" (Lk 8: 39). After another cure, this time of a leper, Jesus told that person, "Go and show yourself to the priest and offer the gift Moses prescribed. That should be the proof they need" (Mt 8, 4). Show forth that greater light and truer love which you now possess in a conscientious, consistent obedience to all the rites and external practices of your religion.

The events of October 9, 1845—the day Newman embraced the Catholic communion—are a good illustration of the elemental difference he saw between feelings and faith. We would expect, after his long, patient search, after the years of doubt and questioning, that Newman's entry into the church would be an emotionally overwhelming experience. Exactly the opposite seems to have been the case; the entries into his personal journal for that day are strangely low-keyed. Down the right-hand side of the page are listed the letters written and received and then, in the lower left-hand corner, there is a small cross followed by the brief statement, "admitted into the Cath. Ch. with Bowles and Stanton."

Earlier that year, in writing to his friend John Keble, Newman had described his approaching conversion by saying, "I am setting my face absolutely towards the wilderness."[5] For he did not feel that either finding Christ or coming to the fullness of faith was a journey from the insecure to the secure or from the

tenuous to the safe, but rather the other way around.
Newman understood the Christian life not in terms of
warm feelings and sensible consolations, but as the
11th chapter of the Epistle to the Hebrews understood it, as a "venture of faith," a journey into the
unknown:

> If then faith be the essence of a Christian
> life . . . it follows that our duty lies in risking
> upon Christ's word what we have for what
> we have not; and doing so in a noble, generous
> way, not indeed rashly or lightly, still without
> knowing accurately what we are doing, not
> knowing either what we give up, nor again,
> what we shall gain; uncertain about our
> reward, uncertain about our extent of sacrifice,
> in all respects leaning, waiting upon Him,
> trusting in Him to enable us to fulfill our own
> vows, and so in all respects proceeding with-
> out carefulness or anxiety about the future.[6]

An incident in the life of Jesus, one narrated by
three of the four Gospels, best summarizes Newman's
understanding of the place of signs and wonders in the
spiritual life. Jesus had left most of his followers
behind and, accompanied by three special friends,
Peter, James and John, had climbed a mountain to
pray. While they were alone on the mountaintop, something happened to Jesus; he underwent a period of
intense self-awareness and an overwhelming sense of the
presence of God. This is how Mark describes what
happened next:

> There in their presence he was transfigured:
> his clothes became dazzlingly white, whiter
> than any earthly bleacher could make them.
> Elijah appeared to them with Moses; and they

were talking with Jesus. Then Peter spoke
to Jesus: "Rabbi," he said, "it is wonderful
for us to be here; so let us make three tents,
one for you, one for Moses and one for Elijah."
He did not know what to say; they were so
frightened. And a cloud came, covering
them in shadow; and there came a voice from
the cloud, "This is my Son, the Beloved.
Listen to him." Then suddenly, when they
looked round, they saw no one with them
any more but only Jesus (Mk 9:2-8).

Until this moment, these friends of Jesus had
known him in his humanity, as a man like themselves.
He had often been hungry, had fished from the same
boat, drunk from the same wineskin and slept on the
shore beside them around the same campfire. But on
the mountaintop, for one blinding moment, the veil was
suddenly pulled aside and Peter, James and John saw
him as he really was—a man possessed by God.

Peter was so overwhelmed by the experience that he
could only say trite words like "wonderful" and make
foolish suggestions that they set up some sort of shrine
to the event, a campsite with three tents. Yet the reason
why Peter and the other two friends were privileged
to share this rare moment in the life of Jesus was not
to erect monuments to the experience, but because they
would soon return to the daily struggles of life. Before
many months passed, they would see Jesus overwhelmed
by events. He would be betrayed by a friend, arrested,
beaten, condemned and finally would suffer public
execution. That moment on the mountaintop was intended to strengthen them against those dark days
ahead—as a memory of who Jesus really was and as a
promise of what he would be at the resurrection.

There is a parallel between the "peak experience" in the life of the Christian and the mountaintop event in the lives of Peter, James and John. There are times of intense emotion in the spiritual journey—a Marriage Encounter, the experience of peace after Holy Communion, a "really good" confession, a religious profession or ordination, a refreshing retreat, a family wedding, a feeling of fellowship at a prayer meeting. These are the rare, rich moments in the spiritual life that draw the human heart to God. It is wonderful to experience them, as it is also a human temptation to pitch tents on the mountaintop and hope that the feelings accompanying these moments will never end.

But the purpose of emotions in the spiritual life is to make a man or woman aware of the presence of the Lord, never to overshadow him. So they soon fade away, leaving only Jesus who leads the way back down the mountain to the daily tasks of life. Indeed, these feelings *must* fade, as the tender blossoms of spring soon fall away to be replaced by the mature fruit of summer. For most people, as for Peter, James and John, it is enough to have experienced those few, fleeting moments and recall them from time to time as reminders of what it can mean to live as a Christian and as hope of what it will mean at the resurrection of the dead.

· As Miss Holmes discovered, Newman had no romantic illusions about the spiritual life. The moments on the mountain are rich, but rare; most Christians live their lives in the valley, faithfully fulfilling the dreary, daily tasks of life:

> Perhaps you will have to labour in darkness afterwards, out of your Saviour's sight, in the home of your own thoughts, surrounded by sights of this world, and showing forth His

praise among those who are cold-hearted.
Still be quite sure that resolute, consistent
obedience, though unattended with high trans-
port and warm emotion, is far more accept-
able to Him than all those passionate longings
to live in His sight, which look more like religion to the uninstructed. At the very best
these latter are but the graceful beginnings
of obedience, graceful and becoming in children, but in grown spiritual men indecorous,
as the sports of boyhood would seem in
advanced years. Learn to live by faith, which
is a calm, deliberate, rational principle, full
of peace and comfort, and sees Christ, and
rejoices in Him, though sent away from His
presence to labour in the world. You will
have your reward. He will "see you again,
and your heart shall rejoice, and your joy no
man taketh from you."[7]

Altar and choir of Newman's church, St. Mary's, Oxford. "Can I wipe out from my memory, or wish to wipe out, those happy Sunday mornings, light and dark, year after year, when I celebrated . . . in my own church of St. Mary's . . . ."

3.

Heart Speaks to Heart

A short walk up the lane from Oriel College, and across High Street, is the University Church of St. Mary-the-Virgin. Newman was vicar of this church from 1828 until 1843. "Can I wipe out from my memory," he wrote after leaving there, "or wish to wipe out, those happy Sunday mornings, light or dark, year after year, when I celebrated . . . in my own Church of St. Mary's; and in the pleasantness and joy of it heard nothing of the strife of tongues which surrounded its walls."[1]

Life at Oxford in the 1830's is far removed, both in time and temperament, from a busy university campus of today, but the opportunities—and the obstacles—for faith are surprisingly similar. The academic world in which Newman ministered, like contemporary society, reflected widely differing value systems and degrees of religious commitment. There were traditionalists among both students and faculty, secular humanists, hedonists, Evangelicals, those belonging to the ecclesiastical establishment, and liberals flirting with the first stirrings of biblical higher criticism. Proclaiming the Word in such a contradictory and conflicting climate, Newman once observed, was like trying to raise the dead.

The differing value systems and the intellectual fads faced by Newman at Oxford University in the 19th century were the first foreshadowings of the kinds of tensions that frequently afflict Christians in today's secular society. In days past, when human life was less complicated, people more or less shared the same values, ascribed the same meaning to the world around them. Their faith commitment was supported by the culture in which they lived; they knew the answers, felt secure in what they believed.

Today's Christian, however, lives in a world where he or she is offered a confusing multitude of choices and many alternative styles of behavior. Newman once wrote that the faith situation of modern man would be one marked by a "contrariety of influence." His words have come true, for many differing value systems and ideologies today claim the sanction of truth; each demands our acceptance and our allegiance: Equal Rights, Ecological Action, Responsible Sex, Baptism of the Spirit, Meaningful Relationships, No-Fault Divorce, The Third World, Abortion on Demand, Liberation Theology, Political Prisoners, Personal Choice.

In a climate of such widely diverse causes and conflicting values, like a wheat field sown with weeds, it is very difficult to find answers. How is it possible, in the midst of such confusion, to sift the true from the false and discern authentic truth? For Newman, the answer was to be found not only in church pronouncements or in ecclesiastical organizations, but through personal influence—by the witnessing of gospel values in the daily lives of Christians. The power of good example, the attraction of unconscious holiness, always remained a basic element in his spiritual teaching. It was the one sure way, Newman believed, to guarantee that God's Word would survive as a Living Word and would be passed on from one person to another, from one generation to the next:

> . . . the attraction, exerted by unconscious holiness, is of an urgent and irresistible nature; it persuades the weak, the timid, the wavering and the inquiring; it draws forth the affection and loyalty of all who are in a measure like-minded; and over the thoughtless . . . multitude it exercises a sovereign compulsory sway . . . though they understand not the principles or counsels of that spirit, which is "born, not of blood, nor of the will of the flesh, nor of the will of man, but of God."[2]

On a Sunday in late January, 1832, Newman chose as his sermon topic, "Personal Influence, the Means of Propagating the Truth." Significantly, he began his homily by quoting the warning of Jesus to his first followers, "Behold, I send you forth as lambs among wolves." For Newman had noticed at Oxford a phenomenon that today's Christian sees on all sides—error almost always seems to have the upper hand. Why is it that evil always seems to triumph, and virtue appears so unattractive?

There are several reasons to explain this apparent advantage of error over truth. First of all, it is so much easier to spread error than it is to affirm truth. People are always more impressed by "ready speech," smooth talk, Newman noted, than they are by either

beauty or truth. To cite one contemporary example:
A prominent guest on a television talk show may have
difficulties establishing lasting personal relationships,
but because the person can talk uninhibitedly about
"sexual freedom," he or she is much more persuasive than
many happily married couples who are faithful to each
other, but find the meaning of fidelity in their lives
too sacred and too special to share so openly.

Newman also noticed that after people have cut
their ethical moorings their manner of expression did
not appear to be bound by the same sense of delicacy or
reverence as those who cherish truth. This, too, can be
considered a certain "advantage" for error. "Men
who investigate in this merely intellectual way, without
sufficient basis and guidance in their personal virtue,
are bound by no fears or delicacy. Not only from dull-
ness, but by preference, they select ground . . . which
a reverent Faith wishes to keep sacred."[3] How appro-
priate his words are when applied to certain health-
informational booklets provided freshmen on some
college campuses—instructional sources in contemporary
society not inhibited by either delicacy or reverence.

There is another process, also occurring frequently
today, which helps us understand the short-term triumph
of evil over good. That is the tendency for authentic
values to be condemned as vice and vice to masquerade
as virtue. "Evil . . . may simulate all kinds of virtue,"
Newman said, "and thus the Arms of Truth are
turned . . . against itself."[4] To illustrate: certain patterns
of sexual activity used to be described as "unnatural";
today all forms of behavior by consenting adults are
tolerated, except one—total abstinence. Chastity, like
a pack of cigarettes, is now labeled as harmful to
health. Yesterday's virtue has become today's vice.

Despite these obstacles, however, values do endure; faith and belief *have* survived in a secular world. How is Divine Truth still able to touch human hearts? "What is that hidden attribute of the Truth," Newman asks, "and how does it act, prevailing, as it does, single-handed, over the many and multiform errors by which it is incessantly attacked?"[5] There are several reasons which explain why truth endures in the face of all impediments.

1. *People Need Permanent Values.* The multiplicity of choices offered by modern life, the confusing patterns of different value systems can be a hindrance to Christian growth. Newman recognized this problem, but he sensed, too, that a future-shocked world would need more than ever the stability provided by faith. Men and women seem to have an intuitive need for structure in religion as well as in life. In a world of change, the sense of permanence found in spiritual values still has a great attraction for many people:

> The changes of human affairs, which first excited and interested, at length disgust the mind, which then begins to look out for something on which it can rely, for peace and rest; and what can then be found immutable and sure, but God's word and promises, illustrated and conveyed to the inquirer in the person of His faithful servants? Every day shows us how much depends on firmness for obtaining influence in practical matters; and what are all kinds of firmness . . . but likenesses and offshoots of that true stability of heart which is stayed in the grace and in the contemplation of Almighty God?[6]

2. *Each Person Has a Special Moment of Truth.* Newman was also aware of what modern psychology

has come to describe as the "peak experience" or "significant moment." There are certain times in people's lives, he noted, when they are unexpectedly touched by truth. That experience usually is triggered by an event, sometimes joyful, sometimes sad, but an intuition or awareness of life's ultimate meaning suddenly breaks into the human consciousness. People see themselves and their lives in a new way, from a different perspective. Sometimes, too, this awareness of Ultimate Truth is accompanied by intense feelings of peace, self-fulfillment and love.

> The strong hour of Truth, which though unheard and unseen by men as a body, approaches each one of that body in his own turn, though at a different time. Then it is that the powers of the world, its counsels, and its efforts (vigorous as they seemed to be . . .), lose ground, and slow-paced Truth overtakes it.[7]

3. *Goodness Is Naturally Attractive.* Truth survives because real holiness is irresistible; it exercises a strange and compelling power over the hearts of men and women:

> . . . men persuade themselves, with little difficulty, to scoff at principles, to ridicule books, to make sport of the names of good men; but they cannot bear their presence, it is holiness embodied in personal form, which they cannot steadily confront and bear down. . . .[8]

Newman's words would explain the powerful influence exerted by the lives of some of the great men and women of our century—people such as John XXIII, Dag Hammarskjold or Mother Teresa of Calcutta.

Rare as such extraordinary examples of holiness may seem,

> They are enough to carry on God's noiseless work. . . . A few highly endowed men will rescue the world for centuries to come. . . . Such men, like the Prophet, are placed upon their watchtower, and light their beacons on the heights. Each receives and transmits the sacred flame, trimming it in rivalry of his predecessor, and fully purposed to send it on as bright as it had reached him; and thus the self-same fire, once kindled in Moriah, though seeming at intervals to fail, has at length reached us in safety, and will in like manner . . . be carried forward even to the end.[9]

The importance of personal influence for the preservation and transmission of religious faith suggests several practical implications for the lives of 20th-century Christians. For example, Newman's words would encourage spiritual directors to examine carefully the use of role-models in the religious formation of adult Catholics. Where are the men and women of today to look for behavior models and guides for mature Christian living? Canonized saints have fulfilled this role to some extent in the past, but who are the flesh and blood examples of what it means to be an adult Catholic in a post-Vatican II church?

The need felt by many people for support from Catholics sharing similar values may also be a reason to explain, in part, the enormous growth of certain contemporary movements within the church such as Marriage Encounter and charismatic prayer groups. If personal influence is such a powerful element in the process of passing on that sacred flame, as Newman believes, then affiliation with those formal or informal groups which promote one-to-one relationships becomes an equally decisive factor in the spiritual life of the Christian.

Newman's insights would also apply to the broader context of religious education, whether offered in a released-time setting or through a parish adult education program. His emphasis on personal influence would suggest a strong cultural-historical approach in such educational endeavors. Students would be encouraged to examine their faith heritage as it has been handed down in the lives of those great men and women of the past who, because of their fidelity to certain traditions and values, were able to transmit that sacred flame far beyond their own time and "rescue their world for centuries to come."

The story of Sir Thomas More and his fidelity to Rome would still have relevance, even in an ecumenical age. St. Benedict and the spiritual riches of Western Monasticism are another example, as is the preservation of their faith by the Irish during the Famine, the exile of French-Canadian Catholics from their homes in Nova Scotia and the story of Mother Cabrini and her work with the Italian immigrants in America at the beginning of the 20th century. Joan of Arc, Athanasius, Edel Quinn, Edmund Campion, Franz Jaggerstatter, Tom Dooley, Elizabeth Seton and John Henry Newman— "these communicate their light to a number of lesser luminaries, by whom, in its turn, it is distributed through the world; the first sources of illumination being all the while unseen even by the majority of sincere Christians— unseen as is that Supreme Author of Light and Truth, from whom all good primarily proceeds."[10]

When religion practices what it preaches, then people will believe. This is the basis for Newman's doctrine on the power of personal influence, and subsequent events in his own life demonstrate the prophetic nature of his teaching. In the 1830's many Oxford Anglicans were growing increasingly curious about Catholic customs and liturgical practices. Some of Newman's own associates were even visiting the newly opened chapel of a nearby Catholic college to hear plainchant and attend High Mass. Newman never attended, for in those days he was not attracted by Roman ways or by Roman worship.

His main criticism of the Church of Rome was its lack of holiness. "I see no marks of sanctity," he wrote in a letter,

> . . . if they want to convert England, let them go barefoot into our manufacturing towns—let them preach to the people like St. Francis Xavier—let them be pelted and trampled on—and I will admit that they can do what we cannot. . . . Let them use the proper arms of the church, and they will prove that they are the church by using them.[11]

Some months before this letter was written, and unknown to Newman at the time, an Italian priest by the name of Dominic Barberi had arrived in England as a missionary. Father Dominic was moved by a strange desire to work for the conversion of England and fulfilled, in his own person, the condition laid down in Newman's letter. The Italian missionary, ignorant of the cultural differences between his homeland and this Protestant country, had begun his mission by walking through the streets of English industrial towns wearing his religious habit and sandals. Father Dominic preached in broken English to everyone who would listen; sometimes he was pelted with mud but, surprisingly, on other occasions people paused to listen.

In 1843, Newman left Oxford and, accompanied by several companions from the university, formed a small community at Littlemore, a nearby village, where in 1836, with financial help from his mother, he had founded a mission church of Oxford. They lived in a row of stone cottages and spent most of their days in study and prayer. It was at Littlemore that Newman began to write his classic work, *An Essay on the Development of Christian Doctrine.*

By 1845, nearly all of Newman's companions had decided to enter the Catholic Church. In late September of that year, John Dobree Dalgairns, one of the first members of the Littlemore community, travelled to Staffordshire to be received into the church by Father Dominic. Several days later, Dalgairns went to Newman's room to tell him that Father Dominic would be passing through Oxford. Newman remarked softly, "When you see your friend, will you tell him that I wish him to receive me into the Church of Christ?"[12]

Father Dominic arrived at Littlemore late that evening and the next day, October 9, 1845, Newman knelt on the stone floor of the Littlemore chapel and was received into the Catholic Church. Newman said of Father Dominic, "His very look had about it something holy. No wonder I became his convert and penitent."[13]

Many years later, when Newman was made a cardinal, he was asked to select a motto for his prelatial coat of arms. He adapted words his favorite composer, Beethoven, had once written on the manuscript of the Mass in D. That motto expressed Newman's lifelong belief in the power of personal influence, *Cor Ad Cor Loquitur*—Heart Speaks to Heart.

The stone cottages in the village of Littlemore, a few miles outside Oxford, where Newman lived in retirement from 1843 until 1846. It was here, on October 9, 1845, that he was received into the Catholic Church by Father Barberi.

4.

Christ Upon the Waters

The Sunday following his reception into the
Catholic Church by Father Barberi, Newman and four
other new converts walked the three miles from Littlemore to attend Mass for the first time at St. Clement's,
the local Catholic chapel. Like other Catholic houses
of worship, St. Clement's was a plain, unobtrusive
building which stood a little back from the road beside
an inn. English Catholics, oppressed by centuries of
persecution and civil sanction, had learned to use terms
such as "prayers" or "duties" as discreet euphemisms
for Mass.

Three hundred years had passed since the days of
the Reformation when the Mass had been forbidden by
law and lay Catholics taxed double for their convictions.
In those days, sons of the Catholic nobility were sent
abroad for study; some were secretly ordained and
returned to their homeland to perform their priestly
ministries with a price upon their heads. Many 16th-
century English Catholics, including Jane Wiseman and

Henry Vaux, were imprisoned because of their religious beliefs; others, like Margaret Clitherow and Edmund Campion, had been martyred for the faith. But the centuries of persecution and repression had finally taken their toll, so that the Catholics who knelt beside Newman at St. Clement's that Sunday in October of 1845 were a tattered remnant of a once vital faith community, "a mere handful of individuals, who might be counted, like the pebbles and *detritus* of the great deluge."[1] Newman would later describe his earliest impressions of English Catholics in this way:

> . . . as we went to and fro, looking with a boy's curious eye through the great city, we might come to-day upon some Moravian chapel, or Quaker's meeting-house, and to-morrow on a chapel of the "Roman Catholics": but nothing was to be gathered from it, except that there were lights burning there, and some boys in white, swinging censers; and what it all meant could only be learned from books, from Protestant Histories and Sermons; and they did not report well of "the Roman Catholics". . . .[2]

The situation of the English Catholic community in the early 19th century was so wretched, Newman felt, that it was almost as if the Lord had set the stage to make the impossible happen; as the prophet Elias, in his celebrated confrontation with the false priests of Baal (1 Kgs 18: 34-37), had deliberately watered down the holocaust as a defiant proof of the power of Yahweh, so:

> [The Lord] . . . put Himself to every disadvantage. He suffered the daily sacrifice to be suspended, the hierarchy to be driven out, education to be prohibited, religious houses

to be plundered and suppressed, cathedrals
to be desecrated, shrines to be rifled, religious
rites and duties to be interdicted by the law
of the land. He would owe the world nothing
in that revival of the Church which was to
follow. He wrought, as in the old time by His
prophet Elias who, when he was to light the
sacrifice with fire from heaven, drenched the
burnt-offering with water the first time, the
second time, and the third time; "and the water
ran round about the altar, and the trench was
filled up with water." He wrought as He
Himself had done in the raising of Lazarus;
for when He heard that His friend was sick,
"He remained in the same place two days":
on the third day He "said plainly, Lazarus is
dead, and I am glad, for your sake, that I was
not there, that you may believe"; and then,
at length, He went and raised him from the
grave.[3]

For almost three centuries, after the Reformation
had dismantled the ecclesiastical structure, there were
no Catholic dioceses, no bishops in England. The church
had been administered from Rome as a missionary
territory without a resident hierarchy, but with priests
acting as bishops who were known as "Vicars Apostolic."
Then, in 1850, five years after Newman's conversion,
new English dioceses were established and local bishops
appointed to meet the needs of the large number of
converts following the Oxford Movement and the flood
of Irish immigrants. One of the Vicars Apostolic,
Nicholas Wiseman, was named Cardinal Archbishop
of Westminster. A newspaper clipping gives an interesting insight into the sudden and phenomenal change in
the religious climate of the times. Newman was reported
to have been at a Catholic parish in Leeds where he
received into the church a "batch of converts" (as the

newspaper account described them)—seven clergymen and 14 lay persons. The group included almost the entire ministerial team from St. Saviour's, a neighboring Anglican parish—two vicars and three curates![4]

Lazarus, in the person of the Catholic community, may have come back from the grave, but Cardinal Wiseman's appointment and the sudden revitalization of the Catholic cause was quickly interpreted as "papal aggression" in Protestant England. The pope was hanged in effigy; *The Times* described Catholic restoration as a "figment of the Papal brain"; priests were pelted with mud on the streets and one Anglican clergyman almost precipitated a riot by declaring from his pulpit that "death alone" should be the answer to Roman Catholic evils.[5]

The times were tense, so when Newman was asked to preach at the installation of the first bishop of the new Diocese of Birmingham, in late October of 1850, he accepted gladly. Newman's homily was entitled "Christ Upon the Waters" and he spoke about the church's role in human history and the reasons why she experiences from time to time the violent storms of prejudice and persecution. He observed that, on at least two occasions, Jesus himself was not recognized even by his disciples who knew and loved him. St. Peter, for example, did not notice Jesus after the resurrection until John pointed out the Lord (Jn 21: 1-7). Moreover, when Jesus came walking toward their boat during that storm at sea, the disciples were at first afraid of him as if he were some evil or malignant specter: ". . . they were terrified. 'It is a ghost!' they said, and in their fear they began to cry out" (Mt 14: 26).

If the Lord's own followers were so dull and insensitive that they failed to recognize his presence, then it should come as no surprise that people at other times, for reasons of ignorance or prejudice, should also be blind to his presence in his church. So it happens that the Christian community, as she makes her way through the centuries, will not only pass unnoticed by some men and women, but will even occasion the hardening of other human hearts against her. For the church, like the Lord himself, ". . . is destined to be the downfall and the rise of many . . . a sign that will be opposed . . ." (Lk 2: 34).

Newman was no stranger to the workings of discrimination and prejudice. During his tenure as vicar of St. Mary's, members of the Oxford faculty had carefully maneuvered him out of positions of influence at the university. Again, while still an Anglican, Newman was accused of "popery" for his defense of Christian tradition in *Tract 90.* His conversion to Catholicism brought magazine articles and letters which raised many questions about the sincerity of his motives, but only rarely considered the reasons behind his choice. So it is not surprising, given the fears and feelings of the times, that in a major portion of his sermon, "Christ Upon the Waters," Newman shares with his Catholic brethren some of his own experience and unique insights into the workings and causes of religious prejudice. His intuitions can be summarized in this way:

1. *Prejudice discredits genuine religious experience.* Jesus worked miracles to convince the incredulous, but some people were able to explain even these signs away by attributing them to the devil: "A possessed man who was brought to him was blind and mute. He cured the man so that he could speak and see. All in the crowd were astonished. 'Might this not be David's son?' they asked. When the Pharisees heard this, they charged,

'This man can expel demons only with the help of Beelzebul, the prince of demons'" (Mt 12: 22-24).

So the Lord warned his first followers, and those who would come after them, that there would be times when their most well-intentioned efforts would be equally misinterpreted: "No pupil outranks his teacher, no slave his master. . . . If they call the head of the house Beelzebul, how much more the members of his household!" (Mt 10: 24-25). Newman describes it in this way:

> Does the Church fulfill the Scripture description of being weak and yet strong, of conquering by yielding, of having nothing yet gaining all things, and of exercising power without wealth or station? This wonderful fact, which ought surely to startle the most obstinate, is assigned, not to the power of God, but to some political art or conspiracy. Angels walk the earth in vain . . . . Good . . . it cannot, shall not be; rather believe anything than that it comes from God.[6]

Contemporary society is too sophisticated to allege that a real demon with a regal title is the cause of Christianity's vitality. Today darker spirits with newer names are invoked to explain away the church's importance in the lives of so many people: *fear, guilt, fanaticism* or *insecurity*. The devil may have changed his name, but for some the Christian community's continuing presence in the world is due not to the power of God, but to the influence of evil:

> There never was a more successful artifice than this, which the author of evil has devised against his Maker, that God's work is not God's but his own. He has spread this abroad in the world, as thieves in a crowd escape by

giving the alarm; and men, in their simplicity,
run away from Christ as if Christ were he,
and run into his arms as if he were Christ.[7]

2. *Prejudice overemphasizes religious failures.* If
the goodness of the church is so easily interpreted as
evil by her enemies, then all the more reason that the
Christian community's real failures in the past and
present will also be exploited to her discredit.

The newspapers of Newman's day had made much
of a bizarre story involving a convert American clergyman, the Reverend Pierce Connelly, and his wife,
Cornelia. After their conversion, Connelly persuaded
his wife to enter the convent to clear his way for ordination as a Catholic priest. Later he became dissatisfied,
converted back to Protestantism and asked his wife to
rejoin him. When Cornelia Connelly refused, in the
meantime having founded a new congregation of teaching sisters in England, the Reverend Connelly brought
a civil suit against her for the restoration of his
conjugal rights.

Newman certainly must have had just this sort of
public scandal in mind when he observed that, while
the church has good children, she has also mothered
those who are wayward. God might have formed a per-
fect church; he chose, instead, to establish one that was
human. Jesus predicted that the weeds, sown by the
enemy, would remain with the wheat until the harvest
at the end of the world (Mt 12: 24-29). He also stated
that his church would be like a fisherman's net, gather-
ing in every kind and not sorted out until evening
(Mt 13: 47-50).

However, if scandal is the exception rather than
the rule in religion, the question remains to be asked

as to why there are people who will turn away from the church because of the hypocrisy of only a few of her members. Newman used an inspired example, based upon the public transportation of his day, to answer that difficulty. He said that a scandal in the church is like an occasional disastrous train wreck. The catastrophe is so enormous that its emotional impact upon certain travelers is beyond all reason; some people are so overwhelmed by the tragedy that they determine never to ride the train again.

A commercial airline crash is a contemporary illustration of Newman's insights into the effects of scandal. Most people, when they hear of a disaster, are saddened by the loss of life, but then think about the great number of planes flying every day, the high safety record of the airlines and the relatively small number of fatal crashes. They calculate that flying the continent is statistically safer than driving home on the expressway! But there are always a few men and women whose imagination is more active than their common sense. They are so overwhelmed by the catastrophe that they don't consider the percentages; they decide never to fly.

So it is with scandals in religion. Some people are so overwhelmed by the exceptions that they are unable to consider calmly the whole of religion. They focus on some personal or public failure of "organized religion"—a rigid upbringing, a bad experience in a parochial school, the severity of Irish priests as depicted in popular novels, or mass suicides among members of a religious cult—and decide never to set foot inside a church again.

3. *"Cheap Knowledge" nurtures prejudice.* Early in his career as vicar of St. Mary's, Newman had tactfully declined to witness the wedding of Miss Jubber,

a young resident of Oxford. Her father, a baker, was a religious nonconformist, and had not permitted any members of his family to be baptized. Newman declined to officiate because he sincerely felt that Christian marriage was for baptized Christians.

Miss Jubber was married in another parish, but an inaccurate and highly biased description of the incident, reported first in an Oxford newspaper, was reprinted in *The Times* of London. Soon Newman was bombarded with anonymous letters accusing him of alcoholism and—for the first, but not the last time in his life as an Anglican—of closet papalism.

Although Newman's own books had a wide audience and an enormous influence among educated circles, he was aware that average people had little time and less inclination for theological thought, preferring, instead, to accept their religious opinions passively from popular periodicals and daily newspapers:

> . . . in an age like this, when everyone reads and has a voice in public matters, it is indispensable that they should have persons to provide them with their ideas, the clothing of their mind, and that of the best fashion. Hence the extreme influence of periodical publications at this day, quarterly, monthly, or daily; these teach the multitude of men what to think and what to say. . . . Is it to be supposed that a man is to take the trouble of finding out truth himself, when he can pay for it? So his only object is to have cheap knowledge; that he may have his views of revelation, and dogma, and policy, and conduct—in short, of right and wrong—ready to hand, as he has his tablecloth laid for his breakfast, and the materials provided for the meal.[8]

Today, sources for the diffusion of religious pre-conceptions and misinformation have increased enormously. Television and the cinema have become major vehicles of that "cheap knowledge" so disparaged by Newman. For example, a talk-show host says earnestly, "I believe in caring, and that's what religion is all about!" and his studio audience breaks into spontaneous applause; a television serial depicts a military chaplain as a bungling incompetent and millions of viewers accept that stereotype as the norm. The mass media still disseminate, at times, the most blatant prejudices and distorted interpretations of religious experience.

4. *The roots of prejudice endure.* One reason for the abiding presence of prejudice, in Newman's view, is because most human conduct is interpreted according to its context; actions, in many cases, are good or bad depending upon the situation. There is an endless reservoir of behavior, so when people view the life of the Christian community through prejudiced eyes, they will always find the evidence they need to validate their fundamental viewpoint:

> Day by day, then, as it passes, furnishes, as a matter of course, a series of charges against us, simply because it furnishes a succession of our sayings and doings. Whatever we do, whatever we do not do, is a demonstration against us. Do we argue? men are surprised at our insolence or effrontery; are we silent? we are underhand and deep. Do we appeal to the law? it is in order to evade it; do we obey the Church? it is a sign of our disloyalty. Do we state our pretensions? we blaspheme; do we conceal them? we are liars and hypocrites.[9]

Jesus had also adverted to this aspect of anti-religious prejudice when he compared the people of his day to bored and restless children whom no one could ever please:

> What comparison can I use for the men of today? What are they like? They are like children squatting in the city squares and calling to their playmates,
>> We piped you a tune but you did not dance,
>> We sang you a dirge but you did not wail.
>
> I mean that John the Baptizer came neither eating bread nor drinking wine, and you say, "He is mad!" The Son of Man came and he both ate and drank, and you say, "Here is a glutton and a drunkard, a friend of tax collectors and sinners!" (Lk 7: 31-33).

Like the Lord, so his people. Is the contemporary church using the democratic process to lobby for social change? Then she is accused of "mixing religion with politics." If she encourages prayer and the interior life, she is "not speaking out on social issues." The Christian community tries to give direction to people's lives and this behavior is labeled "autocratic"; if men and women are trusted to find their own way religiously, then the church is described as "not giving any answers." Prejudice is thus like the restlessness of a little child which no behavior can ever satisfy.

So with good reason did Newman describe the workings of prejudice and compare the situation facing English Catholics, in the middle of the 19th century, to that of the frightened followers of Jesus tossed about in their little boat during the storm at sea (Mk 6: 45-52).

Although the Apostles had been rowing almost all night long, they were unable to make any progress against the strong head winds and were almost at the point of despair. Then, at the darkest hour of the night, they saw the Lord walking toward them on the water. "It is I," he said, "do not be afraid." The winds died and the boat reached shore.

Newman, because of his studies of the church of the first few centuries, had a comprehensive view of the life of the Christian community. Not only was he sensitive to the church's successes and failures in the 19th century, but he had seen her face in the 5th century when Christianity was emerging from the age of persecution to a world that was no longer pagan. Before Newman died, almost at the threshold of the 20th century, he would look to the future and see again the features of that same community as she was evolving into a "post-Christian" world.

From this rich perspective, Newman was aware that the church, as she makes her pilgrim way through human history, is constantly reliving in her life the gospel rhythms of death and resurrection; she is always being delivered over to the death of Jesus, only to rise again, so that "the life of Jesus may also be revealed" (2 Cor 4: 10).

> Scarcely are we singing *Te Deum*, when we have to turn to our *Misereres;* scarcely are we at peace, when we are in persecution; scarcely have we gained a triumph, when we are visited by a scandal. Nay, we make progress by means of our reverses; our griefs are our consolations; we lose Stephen to gain Paul, and Matthias replaces the traitor Judas.[10]

So it has always been with the church that the Lord who was able to walk on the waters could also ride triumphantly over the tumultuous events of history, over the fickle billows of human hearts and human prejudices:

> Who can say why so old a framework, put together eighteen hundred years ago, should have lasted, against all human calculation, even to this day; always going, and never gone; ever failing, yet ever managing to explore new seas and foreign coasts—except that He, who once said to the rowers, "It is I, be not afraid," and to the waters, "Peace," is still in His own ark which He has made, to direct and to prosper her course? . . .
>
> It is the Lord from heaven, who is our light in the gloom, our confidence in the storm. There is nothing hard to Him who is almighty; nothing strange to Him who is all-manifold in operation and all-fruitful in resource. The clouds break, and the sun shines, and the sea is smooth, in its appointed season.[11]

Newman's desk in the Littlemore cottage chapel. He wrote *The
Development of Christian Doctrine* on this writing table and
Father Barberi used the desk as an altar for Mass following
Newman's entry into the Catholic Church.

5.

Divine Calls

Newman's decision to enter the Catholic Church, unlike the conversion stories of St. Paul and St. Augustine, did not come suddenly. Sometimes people will change the direction of their lives while reading a book, hearing a sermon or after a profoundly transforming religious experience. Not so with Newman. He was the same person and believed the same way the morning after he entered the church as the morning before. "I was not conscious to myself," he said, "on my conversion of any change, intellectual or moral, wrought in my mind. I was not conscious of firmer faith in the fundamental truths of Revelation, or of more self-command; I had not more fervour; but it was like coming into port after a rough sea."[1]

Newman's conversion came about gradually, almost imperceptably, the result of his fidelity to many little "calls" from God to which he had responded his whole life long. By answering these loving invitations from the Lord, which came to him through prayer, study and the circumstances of his life, Newman was able to recover the fullness of the Christian faith.

So Newman understood a call from God in a very special way. For him, such an invitation from the Lord was different from a "vocation" where a person changes the external circumstances of his or her life. Such would be the case in a decision to marry or a choice to enter a contemplative community. In Newman's meaning of call, the externals of life remain much the same as before, but because of a person's acceptance of God's invitation, he or she is raised internally to a new consciousness, a new level of spiritual awareness.

Nor is it necessary, Newman believes, that a person be consciously aware, at the time, that God is calling him or her. For it frequently happens that men and women will look back over a certain portion of their lives and only then are struck by the way their values have undergone a subtle, but significant development. They sense within their hearts, for example, an awareness of a greater need for prayer and self-discipline, a deeper tolerance for the failings of others, a new appreciation of the role of scripture and the Eucharist in their lives. Their values may have even changed about the very meaning of life itself. These changes take place, Newman says, because people have responded to God's calls, sometimes without even being aware of the process, and are led forward to a greater awareness of life and a deeper love of Christ.

During his lifetime, the Lord called people by his voice and visible presence; he calls us today in two ways. *Internally,* we are led by what Newman called our "kindly light," conscience; *externally,* we can also discern his call in the circumstances of our daily lives. Of the many external events in life, Newman felt that there are some special situations where God's loving presence is particularly evident. Here are a few he mentions:

Friendship. At Oriel College in 1826, Newman met for the first time a brilliant young scholar, Richard Hurrell Froude. Froude succumbed to tuberculosis a decade later, but not before he and Newman had become close friends. Froude shared Newman's spiritual sensitivities and hunger for holiness, but his theological background, at that time, was much richer than Newman's. As a result of his friendship and conversations with Froude, Newman began to shed some of his Evangelical prejudices against Rome, acquired a sense of reverence for the Blessed Virgin Mary and gradually came to believe in the Real Presence of Christ in the Eucharist.

Newman describes the way God can call us through our friends:

> We get acquainted with someone whom God
> employs to bring before us a number of truths
> which were closed on us before; and we but
> half understand them, and not half approve
> of them; and yet God seems to speak in them,
> and Scripture to confirm them. This is a case
> which not unfrequently occurs, and it
> involves a call to follow on to know the Lord.[2]

Today it may be a college roommate, a neighbor, a marriage partner or a new associate at work who, all unwittingly, becomes God's voice to us. By their humanity, or their care, they help raise our eyes to new dimensions of life, to a new awareness of reality.

The Loss of Someone We Love. Mary Newman was John's youngest sister. She was his favorite and

wrote him laughing, teasing letters. At the end of the
Christmas holidays, early in 1828, Mary was taken ill
and died quite suddenly. She had just turned 19. Her
death was a stunning blow to her brother and ever after-
ward he could never speak of Mary without weeping.
But as Newman later explained, he saw a particular
providence in his sister's loss, "The truth is, I was
beginning to prefer intellectual excellence to moral; I
was drifting in the direction of the Liberalism of the
day. I was rudely awakened from my dream . . . by
two great blows—illness and bereavement."[3]

Newman most certainly had his sister Mary's death
in mind when he described the way the Lord also
speaks to us through the death of a loved one:

> Perhaps it may be the loss of some dear friend
> or relative through which the call comes to
> us; which shows us the vanity of things below,
> and prompts us to make God our sole stay.
> We through grace do in a way we never did
> before; and in the course of years, when we
> look back on our life, we find that that sad
> event has brought us into a new state of faith
> and judgment. . . . We thought, before it
> took place, that we were serving God, and so
> we were in a measure; but we find that, what-
> ever our present infirmities may be, and how-
> ever far we be still from the highest state of
> illumination, then at least we were serving the
> world under the show and belief of serving
> God."[4]

Most of us can accept the inevitability of death,
but the loss of a loved one, a parent or dear friend, still
brings its own special call from God. For a moment we
are brought face to face with the meaning, not only of
the lives of those we loved, but of our own lives as well;

we decide, all over again, what is important to us and choose anew the direction we wish our lives to take.

Significant Moments. Then those events occur which are somehow "bigger than life." They touch us at the deepest level of our being and we are forced, by the course of circumstances, to affirm or deny certain values we have always accepted, but have never before really examined or made our own.

There were many such threshold experiences in Newman's life, but the one that influenced him the most and ultimately led to the beginning of the Oxford Movement started off as a political act, the Parliamentary Reform Bill of 1832. This law suppressed 10 inactive Anglican dioceses and a few bishoprics in Ireland. Some Englishmen, perhaps even the lawmakers themselves, saw the legal act as merely a routine administrative move by the government; Newman, however, viewed the Parliamentary action as the first step in the secularization of the church by the state. Was the church merely a department of government, Newman asked in his *Tracts for the Times,* or was it a divine institution and its bishops successors of the Apostles? People, especially the clergy, were called to choose.

Newman described it this way:

> . . . Perhaps something occurs to force us to take a part for God or against Him. The world requires of us some sacrifice which we ought not to grant to it. Some tempting offer is made us; or some reproach or discredit threatened us; or we have to determine and avow what is truth and what is error. We are enabled to act as God would have us act; and we do so in much fear and perplexity. We do not see our way clearly; we do not see what is to follow from what we have done, and

how it bears upon our general conduct and opinions: yet perhaps it has the most important bearing. That little deed, suddenly exacted of us, almost suddenly resolved on and executed, may be as though a gate into the second or third heaven—an entrance into a higher state of holiness, and into a truer view of things than we have hitherto taken.[5]

There are many contemporary examples of these threshold experiences which involve our basic values and, by forcing us to make a choice, offer the opportunity to enter into a deeper Christian life: An employer's request that we work unnecessary hours on Sunday, an unexpected pregnancy, military conscription for an immoral war, a dehumanizing fraternity initiation, a picket line against unjust working conditions. In all these situations, and a thousand similar ones, we are called to affirm what is true and what is false. The Lord's call is revealed to us in the significant moments of our lives.

Scripture. Newman also describes how God's word can be a stimulus to change in our lives.

We may be in the practice of reading Scripture carefully, and trying to serve God, and its sense may, as if suddenly, break upon us, in a way it never did before. Some thought may suggest itself to us, which is a key to a great deal in Scripture, or which suggests a great many other thoughts. A new light may be thrown on the precepts of our Lord and His Apostles. We may be able to enter into the manner of life of the early Christians . . . which before was hidden from us, and into the simple maxims on which Scripture bases it. We may be led to understand that it is very different from the life which men live now.

Now knowledge is a call to action: an insight
into the way of perfection, is a call to perfection.[6]

So God's call can come suddenly, as in the lives of
some of the saints, or gradually, as in the case for many
Christians today, through scripture, friendship, the
loss of a loved one, in the significant moments of life.
Whatever way a person receives the Lord's invitation,
Newman felt that there were certain common elements
in all such calls. In his sermon, "Divine Calls," he
identified these factors and showed how they apply
in our spiritual lives:

I. *The Call Is Urgent.* In the 22nd chapter of
Acts, where Paul is describing the events of his conversion, he relates how he heard a voice and answered
with the words, "What is it I must do, sir?" Later on,
in the 26th chapter, when he is telling King Agrippa
about the vision, Paul says substantially the same thing,
"I could not disobey that heavenly vision" (Acts 26: 19).
The lesson is clear: God's calls should be answered
promptly.

This seems to be the case for many of the other
calls described in scripture, especially those we read
about in the New Testament. For example, we read
of the Apostles that as Jesus "was walking along the
Sea of Galilee he watched two brothers, Simon now
known as Peter and his brother Andrew casting a net
into the sea. They were fishermen. He said to them,
'come after me and I will make you fishers of men.'
They *immediately* abandoned their nets and became his
followers" (Mt 4: 18-20).

A little later on, when Jesus saw James and John
with their father, "He called them, and *immediately* they

abandoned boat and father and followed him" (Mt 4: 21-22). The same response with the same sense of urgency characterized the call of the tax collector: "Leaving everything behind, Levi stood up and became his follower" (Lk 5: 28).

On the other hand, people like the rich young man, who seemed to waver or weigh the consequences, were rebuked for their lack of promptness in obeying. The word is spoken, and if the significant moment is not seized, the opportunity is lost. Jesus almost seems to stride into some people's lives; he comes, he calls, he moves on. Either men follow him, or he summons others farther on down the road: "To another he said, 'Come after me.' The man replied, 'Let me bury my father first.' Jesus said to him, 'Let the dead bury their dead; come away and proclaim the kingdom of God.' Yet another said to him, 'I will be your follower, Lord, but first let me take leave of my people at home.' Jesus answered him, 'whoever puts his hand to the plow but keeps looking back is unfit for the reign of God' " (Lk 9: 59-62).

II. *The Way Is Not Clear.* Another aspect of the divine calls recorded in scripture is that the consequences are obscure, the way ahead is never sure. To illustrate: Abraham, the role-model of all believers, was called from his father's home, but was not told where he was going. "Leave your country, your family and your father's house, for the land I will show you" (Gen 12: 1), said the Lord, and Abraham set out, "not knowing where he was going" (Heb 11: 8). Paul, after he had accepted Jesus, was directed only to go to Damascus where he would receive further instructions, "You will be told what to do" (Acts 9: 6). Not without reason do the scriptures also relate that Paul was blinded by his conversion, had to be led by hand into Damascus and was unable to see for three days.

In another sermon, "Ventures of Faith," Newman speaks movingly of how the Apostles themselves were called into the unknown:

> Generous hearts, like James and John, or Peter, often speak largely and confidently beforehand of what they will do for Christ, not insincerely, yet ignorantly; and for their sincerity's sake they are taken at their word as a reward, though they have yet to learn how serious that word is. "They say unto Him, 'we are able' "—and the vow is recorded in heaven.[7]

Then Newman describes how the same call and the same type of response occur in the daily lives of Christians:

> This is the case of us all at many seasons. First, at Confirmation; when we promise what was promised for us at Baptism, yet without being able to understand how much we promise, but rather trusting to God gradually to reveal it, and to give us strength according to our day. . . . And so again, in various ways, the circumstances of the times cause men at certain seasons to take this path or that, for religion's sake. They know not whither they are being carried; they see not the end of their course; they know no more than this, that it is right to do what they are now doing; and they hear a whisper within them, which assures them, as it did the two holy brothers, that whatever their present conduct involves in time to come, they shall, through God's grace, be equal to it.[8]

III. *The Call Continues.* Newman realized, from the way God had dealt with him and from his knowledge of the lives of many of his contemporaries, that spiritual growth was an ongoing process. Like the germinating seed, it happens slowly, almost imperceptibly, as a person remains faithful to the divine calls he or she receives all life long. Newman describes the process with these words:

> . . . we are not called once only, but many times, all through our life Christ is calling us. He called us first in Baptism; but afterwards also; whether we obey His voice or not, He graciously calls us still. If we fall from our Baptism, He calls us on from grace to grace, and from holiness to holiness, while life is given us.[9]

So Abraham was called from his home, Peter from his nets, Matthew from his office, Nathaniel from his retreat. We are always being called, on and on, from one grace to another, from one moment until the next, obeying one invitation only to have another offered us. The Lord calls us first to justify us and then, again and again, to sanctify and glorify us (Rom 8: 30).

> . . . We are slow to master the great truth that Christ is, as it were, walking among us, and by His hand, or eye, or voice, bidding us follow Him. We do not understand that His call is a thing which takes place now. We think it took place in the Apostles' day; but we do not believe in it, we do not look out for it in our own case. We have not eyes to see the Lord; far different from the beloved Apostle, who knew Christ even when the rest of the disciples knew Him not. When He stood on the shore after His resurrection, and bade them cast the

net into the sea, "that disciple whom Jesus
loved cried out to Peter, 'It is the Lord!' "[10]

In later years, Cardinal Wiseman would take credit
for Newman's conversion. Before he was Archbishop
of Westminster, Wiseman had been rector of the English
College in Rome and a respected scholar. In 1839,
when Newman began to have some slight misgivings
about the Church of England, a friend showed him an
article by Wiseman on the Anglican position. But,
contrary to Wiseman's claim, the arguments did not
make sense to Newman. "I read it," Newman wrote
later of the article, "and did not see much in it."[11]
However, Wiseman had included a chance quotation
from St. Augustine, *"Securus judicat orbis terrarum"*—
the judgment of the whole world cannot be mistaken.
It was for Augustine a simple rule of thumb for resolving
early theological controversies.

In his *Apologia,* Newman tells how Augustine's
words "absolutely pulverized" his own theological position and struck him in a way no other words had ever
done before. "I had seen the shadow of a hand upon
the wall," he said and then added, "He who has seen a
ghost, cannot be as if he had never seen it."[12] Newman
also notes that it was at this same time that he wrote
his sermon on "Divine Calls." He considered it so
important in explaining his own pilgrimage of faith that
he included the final section of that sermon in the
Apologia:

> O that we could take that simple view of
> things, as to feel that the one thing which lies
> before us is to please God! What gain is it
> to please the world, to please the great, nay,
> even to please those whom we love, compared
> with this? What gain is it to be applauded,

admired, courted, followed—compared with this one aim, of "not being disobedient to a heavenly vision?" What can this world offer comparable with that insight into spiritual things, that keen faith, that heavenly peace, that high sanctity, that everlasting righteousness, that hope of glory, which they have, who in sincerity love and follow our Lord Jesus Christ?

Let us beg and pray Him day by day to reveal Himself to our souls more fully, to quicken our senses, to give us sight and hearing, taste and touch of the world to come; so to work within us, that we may sincerely say, "Thou shalt guide me with Thy counsel, and after that recline me with glory. Whom have I in heaven but Thee? And there is none upon earth that I desire in comparison of Thee. My flesh and my heart faileth, but God is the strength of my heart, and my portion for ever.[13]

A doorway, Oriel College, Oxford. Newman was elected a
Fellow of Oriel in 1822, but had to resign from the
college when he became a Catholic.

6.

The Kindly Light

In June of 1862 an English newspaper, the *Lincolnshire Express,* reported that Newman had given up the Catholic faith, was living in Paris and had become a complete skeptic. Newman immediately wrote a stinging rebuttal. Experience had taught him that people were more inclined to believe gossip than truth if "the fist was not shaken in their face."[1]

In the search for religious truth the average person seems to be the most gullible. "They will stop listening to the truth and will wander off to fables," Paul once warned Timothy. So some contemporary creeds, like that of the Universal Life Church, have only one article of faith, a belief in "that which is right and every person's right to interpret what is right."[2] Other men and women base their religious beliefs on a literal reading of the Book of the Apocalypse and find support for these beliefs in such books as *The Late, Great Planet Earth.* Still others, especially at the university

level, having heard the simplicities of too many funda-
mentalists, observed the confusions of too many Christians and listened to too many gurus and teachers of
enlightenment, have put the search for religious truth
on the shelf. "Does anyone really know the answers?"
many ask as they wander off to embrace a broad rela-
tivism that proclaims all religions more or less equal.

After observing at close hand the religious climate
at Oxford and in the England of his day, Newman.
wondered why it was that many ordinary people, through
their own fault or not, were so easily confused and led
astray from revealed religion. To put it another way:
If Christianity is so beautiful and true, then why aren't
more men and women believing Christians?

However difficult the answer to that question,
Newman recognized that there was an even more fundamental objection to religious belief. Granted that many
"average" men and women do not have the time or
inclination to study religion seriously, why is it that
highly educated people, who *do* have the abilities and
skills, are to be found on different sides of many
theological issues? For example, some claim that
scripture is the Word of God; others say it is merely
great literature. Jesus, in one system of belief, is the
Father's only Son; in another, he is just an inspired
religious teacher.

So it is not only the unlettered who become lost
in their search for truth and are entranced by fables, but
the highly educated as well. It even happened in Newman's own family. His younger brother, Frank, had
studied with John Henry at Oxford and, like him, had
also undergone an Evangelical conversion. Frank joined
the Plymouth Brethren, went off as a missionary to
Persia, then drifted through Unitarianism, rationalism,

vegetarianism and skepticism. By the time John was taking his momentous step toward Catholicism, Frank, now a university professor, regarded all religions as a matter of choice and told John that he would be better advised to start his own. "That I could be contemplating questions of Truth and Falsehood," Newman wrote later, "never entered his imagination."[3]

The phenomenon of unbelief was not unique to Newman's day, nor to contemporary America; it was also present in the first century of Christianity, as the epistles to the community of believers at Corinth testify. Paul writes of those for whom the cross of Christ is an absurdity and he describes the spiritually blind among the Corinthian Church not as the lowborn and uneducated, but as the wise men of this world, the scribes and the philosophers.

We should not be surprised, Newman explained, when men of acute minds and high intelligence do not accept the message of the gospel. For the Christian, revelation addresses itself to the human heart, to people's love of truth and goodness, to their need for healing, pardon and peace. Quickness of mind, ready wit, a way with words—all are gifts of a different kind than those directed to the heart. A person may receive one, but not the other:

> This, then, is the plain reason why able, or again, why learned men are so often defective Christians, because there is no necessary connection between faith and ability; because faith is one thing and ability is another; because ability of mind is a gift, and faith is a grace.[4]

A gifted painter like Andrew Wyeth would never

be expected to compose music with the skill of a
Leonard Bernstein; the president of the World Bank
does not necessarily play tennis with the finesse of a
Wimbledon finalist. Each one's talents are different.
In much the same way, great intellectual ability and
spiritual sensitivity are distinct gifts. Just as the grace
of contemplative prayer would never enable a person
to read foreign languages or qualify as an astronaut,
so the most penetrating mind, brilliant intellect or
creative imagination will never, of itself, make us
men and women of faith:

> This should be kept in mind when Christians
> are alarmed, as they sometimes are, on hearing
> instances of infidelity or heresy among those
> who read, reflect and inquire; whereas, how-
> ever we may mourn over such instances,
> we have no reason to be surprised at them. . . .
> A belief in Christianity has hardly more con-
> nection with what is called talent, than it has
> with riches, station, power or bodily strength.[5]

The truth which Jesus proclaimed is directed to
the human spirit, to that part of our being open to the
dimension of ultimacy and transcendence which enfolds
us and gives our lives direction and meaning. His
Word will be heard most clearly by those who are alive
to truth, beauty, justice, peace and love. Wisdom
is justified in her children.

Scripture also seems to imply that those men and
women who deliberately reject truth do so because they
have already chosen, at some deep level of their being,
values other than those which reflect the transcendent.
Such was the case of the rich young man who went
away sad "for he had many possessions" (Mk 10: 22).
And there was Herod, who had married his brother

Philip's wife, and was only "curious" about meeting Jesus (Lk 9: 9). So, too, the case of Felix, the Roman governor who became frightened and told Paul, when the Apostle began speaking to him about uprightness, self-control and the coming judgment, "I'll send for you again when I find time" (Acts 24: 25).

On the other hand, there are many examples in the New Testament of people, already living upright lives and actively seeking truth, who come to the fullness of faith. Nathanael is spoken of as "a true Israelite," with "no guile in him" (Jn 1: 47); Joseph of Arimathea was "upright and holy" (Lk 23: 50); the Ethiopian eunuch was already studying scripture when he asked Philip to explain the passage of Isaiah (Acts 8: 31); Cornelius, the Roman centurian, a man "religious and God-fearing," was "in the habit of giving generously to the people and he constantly prayed to God" (Acts 10: 2). At Antioch, Paul preached to Israelites and those "who reverence our God" (Acts 13: 16); and at Thessalonica a great number of religious Greeks believed (Acts 17: 4). There is much evidence that Jesus and his Apostles found many of their first followers, not chiefly from among open sinners, but from those who were trying, however imperfectly, to obey God. "To those who have, more will be given . . ." (Mk 4: 25).

So the first step on the path to faith begins with a person's generous response to the transcendent values offered by the light of his or her conscience. And as conscience continues to present men and women with successive choices, like markings leading down a forest trail, the human heart is drawn ever closer to God, the goal of life's journey and the final source of all happiness. Newman was convinced of the important role played by conscience in this process:

. . . this Word within us not only instructs us up to a certain point, but necessarily raises our minds to the idea of a Teacher, an unseen Teacher: and in proportion as we listen to that Word, and use it, not only do we learn more from it, not only do its dictates become clearer, and its lessons broader, and its principles more consistent, but its very tone is louder and more authoritative and constraining. And thus it is, that to those who use what they have, more is given; for, beginning with obedience, they go on to the intimate perception and belief of one God."[6]

Newman viewed conscience in two ways—as an *inner light* and as *personal choice.* Certain factors in our American culture, especially our Puritan tradition of self-sufficiency and Thoreau's ideas in *Civil Disobedience,* have led to our understanding of conscience only as personal choice, as a decision or judgment one makes about right or wrong. As a result, conflicts between conscience and authority are part of our history—Martin Luther King defying discriminatory laws in the name of conscience, young men protesting a Vietnam war as conscientious objectors, couples practicing contraception with the words, "We've got to follow our conscience."

An understanding of conscience as personal choice, as the proximate internal norm of morality, had always been fundamental to Newman's theological beliefs. He gave his most brilliant exposition of this aspect of conscience in a long letter called *Letter to the Duke of Norfolk,* which he wrote a few years after the 1870 definition of papal infallibility by the First Vatican Council.

Very extravagant claims had been made for the

role of the pope in the church by a small, but powerful group of English Catholics. For example, Cardinal Manning is supposed to have said that he hoped the pope would now define all beliefs and resolve all questions, once and for all, with an infallible decree. W. G. Ward, a prominent writer and lay theologian, announced he would like an infallible pronouncement delivered to his breakfast table every day with the morning paper! Not only was the faith of many average Catholics shaken by these extremes, and other inaccurate rhetoric, but Anglicans were hurt and angered.

Among the critics was Prime Minister William Gladstone, who published a pamphlet accusing English Catholics of disloyalty to their country because they owed blind obedience to the pope. Newman answered the charges in the *Letter to the Duke of Norfolk*. He wrote with great reverence about obedience to religious authority as the ordinary way for Catholics, but took care to point out that obedience should never be blind and that, ultimately, conscience was supreme. Newman then used two delightful examples to make his point. Suppose the pope ordered all the priests of England to give up drink or decreed that there be a lottery in every English parish. What was the recourse for a particular priest who liked wine or felt in his heart that gambling was a sin? Here is how Newman resolved it:

> . . . if the Pope told the English bishops to order their priests to stir themselves energet- ically in favor of teetotalism, and a particular priest was fully persuaded that abstinence from wine was practically a Gnostic error, and therefore felt he could not so exert himself without sin; or suppose there was a Papal order to hold lotteries in each mission for

some religious object, and a priest could say in God's sight that he believed lotteries to be morally wrong, that priest in either of these cases would commit a sin *hic et nunc* if he obeyed the Pope, whether he was right or wrong in his opinion. . . .[7]

Newman's conclusion to his letter is also very enlightening:

I add one remark. Certainly, if I am obliged to bring religion into after-dinner toasts (which indeed does not seem quite the thing) I shall drink—to the Pope, if you please— still, to conscience first, and to the Pope afterwards.[8]

However brilliant Newman's defense of human freedom is, it should be noted that he did not view conscience only as personal choice. His understanding of the light within is far richer and much more profound than the way it has been interpreted by civil libertarians. The role of conscience, Newman believed, was to offer us an interior light by which we would not only become more and more sensitive to the presence of God within our hearts, but would be led to a more intimate union with him, as well as to help us sort out right and wrong and assert ourselves against injustice.

This is a subject which cannot too strongly be insisted upon. Act up to your light, though in the midst of difficulties, and you will be carried on, you do not know how far. Abraham obeyed the call and journeyed, not knowing whither he went; so we, if we follow the voice of God, shall be brought on step by step into a new world, of which before we had no idea. This is His gracious way with us: He gives, not all at once, but by measure and season, wisely.[9]

Newman was very concerned that conscience be understood as the "voice of God." It was not only that obedience to his "kindly light" had led him to take the momentous steps in his own life—despite the loss of university position, public reputation and the affection of his family and friends—but he knew that obedience to conscience as the voice of God would lead to obedience to the gospel as the Word of God. For fidelity to a personal request is far more demanding than loyalty to abstract ethical principles.

One of Newman's novels, *Callista,* is the story of third-century Christians during the great persecution of the Emperor Decius. The book's beautiful heroine, a young pagan woman, describes her inner voice in this way:

> I feel that God within my heart. I feel myself in His presence. He says to me "Do this: don't do that." You may tell me that this dictate is a mere law of my nature, as to joy or to grieve. I cannot understand this. No, it is the echo of a person speaking to me. Nothing shall persuade me that it does not ultimately proceed from a person external to me. It carries with it its proof of its divine origin. My nature feels toward it as towards a person. When I obey it, I feel a satisfaction; when I disobey, a soreness—just like that which I feel in pleasing or offending some revered friend . . . an echo implies a voice; a voice a speaker.[10]

Sensitivity to God's presence can reorient the direction of a person's whole life and have enormous consequences in his or her quest for happiness. But is this inner "voice" a reality or only a Victorian cleric's way of describing what modern psychology now calls

guilt feelings or auditory hallucinations? Newman was
well aware of psychological states such as neurotic
guilt and free-floating anxiety (which he called
"fidgets"), but he saw our overwhelming awareness,
commanding insights and sudden promptings in terms
of their ultimate origin; they were, in Callista's beautiful
phrase, but "the echo of a person speaking to me."
These feelings have their source in an inescapable
"Someone":

> Inanimate things cannot stir our affections;
> these are correlative with persons. If, as is
> the case, we feel responsibility, are ashamed,
> are frightened at transgressing the voice of
> conscience, this implies that there is One to
> whom we are responsible, before whom we are
> ashamed, whose claims on us we fear. . . .
> These feelings in us are such as require for
> their exciting cause an intelligent being: we
> are not affectionate towards a stone, nor do
> we feel shame before a horse or a dog; we
> have no remorse or compunction on breaking
> mere human law; yet, so it is, conscience
> excites all these painful emotions, confusion,
> foreboding, self-condemnation and on the
> other hand it sheds upon us a deep peace, a
> sense of security, a resignation, and a hope,
> which there is no earthly object to elicit.[11]

In the spring of 1833, on the eve of the Oxford
Movement, Newman was visiting Italy with some friends.
In April, his companions returned to England, but
Newman went on alone to Sicily for a few more weeks
of travel. He contracted a fever, came close to dying,
but was nursed back to health by his Italian guide. As
he lay delirious in a flea-infested inn, Newman was
filled with feelings of self-reproach about his life. At
the same time he was overwhelmed by an intense aware-

ness of God's forgiving love. He kept repeating over and over, "I have not sinned against the light."[12]

Many reasons might explain the unusual circumstances and events of Newman's life, especially the direction of his spiritual pilgrimage: his extraordinary intellectual talents and educational opportunities, his emotional maturity and rich personal relationships, or his study of the Early Fathers and disenchantment with the established church. If one reason can be offered before all others, however, then surely it must be found in his own understanding of the meaning of that phrase, "I have not sinned against the light."

Obedience to the light of his conscience, despite overwhelming obstacles and in the face of enormous opposition, is the hallmark of his sanctity. By fidelity to that "echo" of the voice within, Newman was led, step by step, from skepticism to faith, as he rediscovered the fullness of the Christian revelation. How simple, and yet how profound a summary of the spiritual life is contained in that phrase, "I have not sinned against the light."

On his way back to England after recovering from the fever, Newman's boat was becalmed for a week off the coast of Sardinia. It was here, looking across the still waters, that he penned the immortal words of his hymn, "Lead Kindly Light." It was, at the same time, a prayer of gratitude for his healing and a prophetic glimpse at the pattern of his whole life:

> Lead, kindly light, amid the encircling gloom,
>   Lead Thou me on!
> The night is dark, and I am far from home—
>   Lead Thou me on!
> Keep Thou my feet; I do not ask to see
> The distant scene; one step enough for me. . . .

Bronze tablet, at No. 86 St. Stephen's Green, Dublin, commemorates Newman's efforts to establish the Catholic University of Ireland.

7.

Discipleship and Disappointments

Macmillan's Magazine, early in 1864, carried a book review by Charles Kingsley, a professor of history at Cambridge. Kingsley, a social activist, novelist and clergyman, had never made Newman's acquaintance, but he used his article as the opportunity for a personal attack:

> Truth, for its own sake, had never been a virtue with the Roman clergy. Father Newman informs us that it need not, and, on the whole, ought not to be. . . .[1]

Newman wrote to *Macmillan's* demanding an immediate retraction; Kingsley replied in the next issue with a statement that sounded like an apology, but still implied that Newman was a liar. Further letters were exchanged and then, shortly after Easter, Newman began to compose a long defense of his life and religious ideals. Sometimes he wrote as many as 16 hours a day; once he was at his writing desk for 22 hours straight.[2]

When he finally laid down his pen two months later, the result was a classic of autobiographical writing, Newman's *Apologia Pro Vita Sua*.

The book was an instant success; public opinion, which had either ignored or remained hostile to Newman since his conversion to Catholicism some 20 years before, now began to change in his favor. Congratulations poured in on all sides. Catholics at last began to sense his genius and the great personal cost of his conversion; many of Newman's old Anglican friendships were renewed. Kingsley, now publicly discredited, suffered a nervous collapse and left for a long rest in Spain.[3]

Muriel Spark, the English novelist and convert, has described the *Apologia* as "the saddest love story in the world."[4] Newman's autobiography is the narrative of one man's fidelity to his religious ideals, first in the Anglican Church, then in the Roman Catholic, despite overwhelming afflictions and disappointments. Another source of information as to the kinds of sufferings experienced by Newman can be found in his *Journal,* or personal diary, where he often confided his deepest feelings. One entry, written in January of 1863, and about a year before the Kingsley attack, suggests some of the interior struggles Newman experienced after his conversion:

> O how forlorn and dreary has been my course since I have been a Catholic! here has been the contrast—as a Protestant, I felt my religion dreary, but not my life—but, as a Catholic, my life dreary, not my religion ... Persons who would naturally look towards me, converts who would naturally come to me, inquirers who would naturally consult me, are stopped by some light or unkind word said against me.[5]

Many years earlier, in a sermon preached at St. Mary's, Newman had drawn a vivid picture of the kinds of trials endured by some of the great Jewish prophets. He used as his frame of reference the sufferings of God's servants mentioned in the *Letter to the Hebrews* where the author states that these prophets

> endured mockery, scourging, even chains and imprisonment. They were stoned, sawed in two, put to death at sword's point; they went about garbed in the skins of sheep or goats, needy, afflicted, tormented. The world was not worthy of them. They wandered about in deserts and on mountains, they dwelt in caves and in holes of the earth (Heb 11: 36-38).

For Newman, Elijah, the prophet who lived in the wilderness, and the hundred prophets whom Obadiah fed in a cave were examples of prophetic wanderers. Micaiah, who was tormented by an idolatrous king, was a prophet who suffered "chains and imprisonment." Isaiah, according to one tradition, was executed by a wooden saw and Zechariah was stoned to death "between the temple and the altar" (Mt 23: 35).

Of all the persecuted prophets in Israel, however, none experienced more of life's afflictions or suffered more interiorly than did the great Jeremiah. The lives of other prophets were examples of homeless wanderings, violent persecution and patient endurance, but Jeremiah's life is the story of a man's fidelity to the Lord's call despite personal rejection and unexpected failures.

Jeremiah's ministry, it seemed to Newman, had passed through three successive stages best summarized by the words, *Great Hopes, Hard Works, Crushing Disappointments*. Without realizing it at the time he

was preaching his sermon on disappointments, Newman
was actually describing the future seasons of his own
ministry and, in some ways, the spiritual "passages"
of many religious and lay people today.

No Old Testament prophet ever commenced his
labors with *greater hopes* than Jeremiah. Like Samuel,
the first prophet, Jeremiah was of the tribe of Levi,
dedicated from his birth to religious service and graced
with an intuitive sense of the presence of the Lord.
"Before I formed you in the womb I knew you," Yahweh
told Jeremiah, "before you came to birth I consecrated
you; I have appointed you as prophet to the nations"
(Jer 1: 5).

Neither did any prophet ever begin his ministry
with higher expectations than Jeremiah. King Josiah,
at most 20 years of age, had succeeded to the throne
and, it seemed, was going to bring about religious re-
forms as had not been experienced since the days of
David, the man after the Lord's own heart. So at first
sight it seemed reasonable for Jeremiah to expect that
the kingdom would prosper and that the Lord's blessings,
which the Jewish remnant were just beginning to enjoy,
would continue.

Pastoral care and special ministries usually start off
with dreams as great as Jeremiah's expectations for
reform at the beginning of his prophetic ministry to
Israel, with hopes as high as Newman's in planning
his many special ministries, but some of these expectations soon proved to be unrealistic; great hopes
often turn into impossible dreams:

> To expect great effects from our exertions for
> religious objects is natural indeed, and inno-
> cent, but it arises from inexperience of the

kind of work we have to do—to change the
heart and will of man. It is a far nobler frame
of mind, to labour, not with the hope of seeing
the fruit of our labour, but for conscience'
sake, as a matter of duty; and again, in faith,
trusting good *will* be done, though we see it
not.[6]

The next phase of discipleship, as Newman under-
stands it, is a period of faithful, but seemingly fruitless,
hard labor for the Lord. Jeremiah's great dreams for
religious reform soon ended with the unexpected death
in battle of the young Josiah. Since the prophet's ministry was carried on for almost 40 years before the
Captivity, Jeremiah's high hopes were deflated early
in his career and he was left to labor on alone without
the visible rewards or public approval that had once
blessed his efforts.

Newman also ministered, for many long years after
his conversion, to a Catholic community that was
unable, for the most part, to appreciate his special
charisms and misinterpreted almost all his efforts. Some
people expected him to begin a crusade to convert
Protestant England, but for Newman, raising the intellectual and spiritual life of Catholics was far more
important than evangelizing Anglicans. Newman's personal priorities were to remedy the deficiencies within
the Roman Catholic Church which were obscuring the
radiance of Christ's face to those outside her membership, and to undertake an intellectual defense of Christianity against a rising tide of secular unbelief. The
church must be prepared for converts, he once said,
as well as converts prepared for the church!

Sometimes, those who labor today in the vineyard
of the Lord expect to reap where they have never sown.

Enthusiasm too easily gives way to discontent when immediate results are not forthcoming. Creative liturgies, for example, take long hours of planning and preparation; but they do not renew a parish overnight. Precious time spent in preparing a high school religion class or a parish council meeting may only begin to bear any real fruit much later. So Christian fidelity to the daily, often dreary tasks of life like committee meetings, home visitation and liturgy planning can sometimes reflect a deeper love and have a more lasting effect in raising the level of faith in a parish than wild enthusiasms and special causes. Some Christians who have never realized that the grain of wheat must die before it produces fruit (Jn 12: 24), that ministry really means much hard work, soon lose heart, have doubts about their vocations, or abandon their religious ideals. Newman, on the other hand, had understood early in his life the biblical ideal about putting one's hand to the hard work of the plow and not looking back:

> Give not over your attempts to serve God,
> though you see nothing come of them. Watch
> and pray, and obey your conscience, though
> you cannot perceive your own progress in
> holiness. Go on, and you cannot but go for-
> ward; believe it, though you do not see it.
> Do the duties of your calling, though they are
> distasteful to you. . . . Let your light shine
> before men, and praise God by a consistent
> life, even though others do not seem to glorify
> their Father on account of it, or to be bene-
> fited by your example. "Cast your bread
> upon the waters, for you shall find it after
> many days. . . . In the morning sow your
> seed, in the evening withhold not your hand;
> for you know not whether shall prosper either
> this or that; or whether they both shall be

alike good." Persevere in the narrow way. The Prophets went through sufferings to which ours are mere trifles; violence and craft combined to turn them aside, but they kept right on, and are at rest.[7]

God's servants, even though they begin with great hopes of success, leading to long hours and dreary days often experience *crushing disappointments* in their ministries. Not that the Lord's promises, or his loving care, ever fail, as Newman explains, but the example of his faithful followers seems to demonstrate that the time for reaping what we have sown is usually not here, but hereafter. Moses, for instance, began by leading the Israelites out of Egypt in triumph; he ended an old man, before his journey was completed, and was only granted a distant glimpse of the Promised Land. Samuel's ministry ended with the people aping pagan ways and choosing a king like the nations around them. Elijah, after his initial success, fled from Jezebel into the wilderness to mourn his disappointments.

Jeremiah's life is also the record of a person passing from hopes to disappointments in the service of the Lord. After the early death of Josiah, Jeremiah was afflicted by persecution from all sides. At one time scripture tells of the people conspiring against him (Jer 18: 18); on another occasion, Jeremiah was seized by the priests and false prophets to be put to death and was only saved by the intervention of certain princes and elders still faithful to the memory of King Josiah (Jer 26: 16).

King Zedekiah had Jeremiah put into prison at a later date (Jer 20: 2) and when the Chaldean army was besieging Jerusalem, Jeremiah was accused of attempting to desert to the enemy, was arrested and then thrown into the muddy bottom of an unused well where he almost starved to death (Jer 38: 6-9). When Jerusalem was finally captured, Jeremiah was carried off into Egypt by men who pretended to treat him respectfully, but then, it is believed, brought him to a violent end. These were a few of the disappointments, the blighted hopes of a gentle and peaceful man who, almost against his will, was chosen by the Lord to be his emissary, but was rejected by the very people to whom he was sent to minister.

Many of the apostolic activities and religious projects so enthusiastically begun by Newman, during both his Anglican and Catholic days, also ended in failure and disappointment. His plans for academic reform at Oxford, for example, were aborted when the Provost of Oriel no longer assigned him any students and then replaced Newman as a college tutor. Newman's attempts in *Tract 90* to interpret the Thirty-Nine Articles in an Anglo-Catholic sense ran into strong opposition among the Anglican bishops of his day.

Later, after Newman had entered the Catholic Church, he worked hard to establish the Catholic University of Ireland, but the project failed because the Catholic bishops were not ready, either for Newman's enlightened views on education, or for his plan to include lay participation in formulating university financial policies. In 1854, Cardinal Wiseman wrote to announce that Pope Pius IX would name Newman a bishop. The news became public and friends sent, not only letters of congratulations, but gifts of a pectoral cross and an episcopal miter. The bishopric never materialized; the Archbishop of Dublin, working behind the scenes, had written to Rome that Newman's appointment "would not be prudent."[8]

Shortly after Newman began work, at the request of the English hierarchy, on a new English translation of the bible, the project was sidetracked by Cardinal Wiseman for reasons that still remain obscure.

On another occasion he was offered a large parcel of land in Oxford and Newman enthusiastically drew up plans to develop a Catholic Center at the university, staffed by priests who were former Oxford men. The chapel and mission—a plan very close to his heart—was blocked by conservative English Catholics who felt that Catholic students should attend Catholic colleges.

So John Henry Newman's life, like Jeremiah's, was the pilgrimage of a man who passed from great hopes to severe disappointments in the service of the Lord.

After he had entered the Catholic Church, a publisher brought out a French edition of a book from Newman's Anglican days, his *University Sermons*. Newman reread the homilies as they were being translated and later confided in a letter to a friend his amazement that his ideas had not been better received within the Catholic community. "Feelings come upon me which do not often else, but then vividly—I mean the feeling that I have not yet been done justice to. . . . People do not know me—and sometimes they half pass me by."[9]

Several human factors can explain why Newman's greatest creative efforts were sometimes ignored and more often deliberately opposed by his coreligionists—creativity is very threatening to those whose approach to life follows more established patterns, and very free people, such as Newman, sometimes call forth from less gifted persons unconscious fears and irrational hostilities. Newman was as much aware of these primeval drives as any student of contemporary psychology, but he also understood human experience, and especially his own life, at deeper levels of meaning. Jesus had once complained to Philip, "After I have been with you all this time, you still do not know me?" (Jn 14: 8), and so for Newman the events of this life, beneath their surface appearances, also reveal the saving action of the Lord for those who have eyes to see.

So it was that Jeremiah, who was so overwhelmed by misfortune that he could find no earthly consolation for himself, nevertheless was sent by the Lord to comfort another prophet, Baruch (Jer 45). In his ministry of consolation to Baruch, Jeremiah has become the role-model of all those faithful followers of the Lord whose personal disappointments and misfortunes have not only afforded them a precious insight into the sufferings of others, but enabled the Lord, through them, to be the comfort and support of hurting human beings. This special grace, as Newman points out, is itself a source of great consolation to those disciples who have experienced disappointments and failure in their lives:

> Doubtless if we are properly minded, we shall
> be very loth to take to ourselves titles of
> honor. We shall be slow to believe that we
> are specially beloved by Christ. But at least
> we may have the blessed certainty that we are
> made instruments for the consolation of
> others. . . .

> Taught by our own pain, our own sorrow, nay,
> by our own sin, we shall have hearts and
> minds exercised for every service of love
> towards those who need it. We shall in our
> measure be comforters after the image of the

Almighty Paraclete, and that in all senses of
the word—advocates, assistants, soothing aids.
Our words and our advice, our very manner,
voice and look, will be gentle and tranquil-
lizing, as of those who have borne their cross
after Christ. We shall not pass by His little
ones rudely, as the world does. The voice of
the widow and the orphan, the poor and
destitute, will at once reach our ears, however
low they speak. Our hearts will open towards
them; our word and deed befriend them.[10]

Newman's teaching is illustrated by the life of the
Apostle to the Gentiles. The feelings of failure experienced by Paul in his ministry not only helped him to
empathize with the sufferings of others, but he was also
enabled to find an entry into the hearts of people high
and low, Jew and Greek. Paul could persuade because
he himself had experienced doubt and perplexity; he
knew how to console, for his own spirit had also felt
the hand of sorrow. Paul's heart, because it had known
disappointments, was able to adapt itself, like some
finely tuned instrument, to the needs and faith situations
of others. "Who is weak," he asks, "that I am not
affected by it? Who is scandalized that I am not aflame
with indignation? If I must boast, I will make a point of
boasting of my weaknesses" (2 Cor. 11: 29-30). Paul
was aware of the deeper meaning of personal sufferings
and disappointments because earlier in his same letter
he observed that the Lord "comforts us in all our
afflictions and thus enables us to comfort those who are
in trouble, with the same consolation we have received
from him" (2 Cor 1: 4).

In a somewhat similar vein, our Lord reminds
St. Peter, "Simon, Simon! Remember that Satan has
asked for you, to sift you all like wheat. But I have

prayed for you that your faith may never fail. You in turn must strengthen your brothers" (Lk 22: 31-32). "Comfort my people," the Lord seems to say to his dearest friends, "comfort them by the disappointments of your ministry and the afflictions of your discipleship."

Sufferings are not of themselves salvific; they have no inherent power to make men and women holier or more heavenly. Disappointments can cause some people to despair; others who endure affliction without love may be left embittered, and their last state worse than the first. Only in the hands of the Lord and through hearts open to his grace does failure—as that experienced in the story of the prophet Jeremiah and in the life of John Henry Newman—become an instrument of power and healing:

> When a man, in whom dwells His grace, is
> lying on the bed of suffering, or when he has
> been stripped of his friends and is solitary,
> he has, in a peculiar way, tasted of the powers
> of the world to come, and exhorts and con-
> soles with authority. He who has been long
> under the rod of God, becomes God's pos-
> session. He bears in his body marks, and is
> sprinkled with drops, which nature could
> not provide for him. He comes "from Edom,
> with dyed garments from Bozrah," and it is
> easy to see with whom he has been con-
> versing. . . . And they who see him, gather
> around like Job's acquaintance, speaking no
> word to him, yet with confidence, with fellow-
> feeling, yet with resignation, as one who is
> under God's teaching and training for the
> work of consolation towards his brethren.
> Him they will seek when trouble comes on
> themselves; turning from all such as delighted
> them in their prosperity, the great or the
> wealthy, or the man of mirth and song, or of

wit, or of resource, or of dexterity, or of knowledge; by a natural instinct turning to those for consolation whom the Lord has heretofore tried by similar troubles. Surely this is a great blessing and cause of glorying to be thus consecrated by affliction as a minister of God's mercies to the afflicted.[11]

Steeple of Newman's Oxford church — St. Mary the Virgin.
"In 1828 I became Vicar of St. Mary's. It was to me
like the feeling of spring weather after winter."

8.

The Second Spring

Newman left Littlemore a few months after his conversion; for the next 32 years he would see the steeple of St. Mary's, Oxford, and the spires of his beloved university in the distance from train windows, as he travelled between London and Birmingham.

Some of the Oxford Movement converts, although convinced in principle of Catholicism, found the cultural and devotional distance between the Anglican and Roman communions very great. "We must throw ourselves into the system," Newman wrote several of his friends at the time and he began his own new religious life by travelling up and down England, meeting Catholic bishops and laymen and visiting educational centers.

Early in 1846, Archbishop Wiseman invited him to Oscott College, near Birmingham, where he spent several months and experienced the spiritual comfort offered by a Catholic devotional practice, reservation of the Blessed Sacrament:

I am writing next room to the chapel. It is such an incomprehensible blessing to have Christ's bodily presence in one's house, within one's walls, and (it) swallows up all other privileges and destroys, or should destroy, every pain. To know that *He* is close by— to be able again and again through the day to go in to Him . . . It is *the* place for intercession surely, where the Blessed Sacrament is.[1]

Some Catholic devotions were a great comfort, but Newman found other aspects of his new life very disconcerting. Much later he described some of these early difficulties:

How dreary my first year . . . when I was the gaze of so many eyes at Oscott, as if some wild incomprehensible beast, caught by the hunter, and a spectacle for Dr. Wiseman to exhibit to strangers, as himself being the hunter who captured it! I did not realize this at the time except in its discomfort; but also, what I did realize, was the strangeness of ways, habits, religious observances, to which, however, I was urged to conform without any delicacy towards my feelings. . . . I was made an humiliation at my minor orders and at the examination for them; and I had to stand at Dr. Wiseman's door waiting for confession amid the Oscott boys. I did not realize these as indignities at the time, though, as I have said, I felt their dreariness.[2]

Newman also began to consider his own role in the church and made up his mind to prepare for the priesthood. The church of Rome would not accept his Anglican orders, a point that caused him much pain. But he accepted the decision more easily when told that the church reordained Catholic priests if there was any doubt as to the validity of their orders. At Wiseman's suggestion Newman went to Rome, accompanied by several other Littlemore converts, to enter the seminary. He would fall asleep during lectures in fundamental theology, so he soon gave up formal classes for private study. Newman's first inclination was to join a teaching order such as the Jesuits or Dominicans; he decided, however, that membership in the Oratory, a less formal association of priests founded by St. Philip Neri, was more suitable for his age (he was 45) and future plans. Newman was ordained a Catholic priest on the first of June, 1847, and later that year returned to England to begin a ministry among the poor in the industrial city of Birmingham.

An unused gin distillery in the middle of a factory district was converted by Newman into a chapel or "oratory" with a library and accommodations for the staff of priests. The Birmingham Oratory was Newman's "home" for the rest of his life. Over 500 people crowded into the chapel for the first Sunday evening services and the Oratorians, fearing an anti-Catholic riot, sent for the police. Newman's sermon, preached in simple language on sin and salvation, soon calmed the suspicions of his new congregation.

The priests of the Birmingham Oratory received an even greater surprise a few days later when, like a scene out of Dickens, their midweek evening classes were flooded with neighborhood urchins. Little boys and girls, the ragtag refuse of the industrial revolution, lived in rat-infested flophouses and worked from dawn until dusk in local factories. Some of these children were as young as seven; they were attracted to the new chapel, as Newman described it, like "herrings in season."[3] He would have liked to open a school, but the children needed work in order to survive, so the Oratorians undertook religious instructions and started a choir for the factory girls. Newman, as he did most of his life, worried about money. The year was 1849, time of the Gold Rush in the American West, and Newman wrote, "O, for a private California!"[4]

A few years after Newman began his ministry to the poor in Birmingham, the Catholic hierarchy was reestablished in England and diocesan bishops appointed by Rome after a lapse of 300 years. A violent anti-Catholic reaction occurred; riots took place in several cities and a few Catholic chapels were burned to the ground. Newman began a series of public lectures to dispel popular prejudices and correct misunderstandings about Catholic belief and practice. These talks were later published as *The Present Position of Catholics in England*.

Even as an Anglican, Newman's calm, more thoughtful approach to religion had been an irritant to the fundamentalist Christians of his day who thought of salvation more in terms of a single, highly emotional experience.

The Protestant Alliance, an evangelical organization, had been sponsoring a series of anti-Catholic lectures throughout England by an ex-priest, Dr. Giacomo Achilli. Achilli, a former member of the Dominican Order, had been defrocked and jailed in Italy for the seduction of several young women. In order to dilute the positive effects of Newman's lectures, Achilli's evangelical sponsors invited him to speak in Birmingham and the former monk was soon telling lurid tales of monastery life.

Cardinal Wiseman possessed documents he had obtained from Italy which revealed the true facts in the

Achilli case and proved that the man was a charlatan. On the basis of Wiseman's evidence, Newman felt secure in exposing Achilli's fraud in a public lecture. Achilli sued for libel, the case went to court and when Newman needed the evidence to substantiate his accusations, Wiseman had misplaced the documents. He found them only later when they were no longer of any use to Newman. After a public trial Newman was found guilty, fined 100 pounds and was lectured by the judge for half an hour on his moral deterioration.

In July of 1851, Archbishop Paul Cullen, representing the Irish hierarchy, called on Newman at the Birmingham Oratory. Archbishop Cullen had met Newman a few years earlier in Rome and now told him that the Irish bishops were concerned about Catholic education in Ireland. Catholics had been unable to attend Trinity College, the only university in Ireland, because the Anglican faith and practice had been obligatory for its students. This requirement had been abolished in 1792, but Catholics were still excluded from fellowships and student grants. So the Irish bishops planned to establish a new Catholic university and Cullen asked Newman to be the new university's first rector.

Newman kept his responsibility as head of the household in Birmingham, and though he lived in Ireland for the next six years, he would frequently return to England. He began his task as rector in May 1852 with a series of Dublin lectures on higher education. These talks were later published as *The Idea of a University,* a classic of educational theory and English prose; they reflected, not only Newman's plans for the new university and his educational experiences at Oxford, but his personal ideas as to the nature and purpose of higher education. An interesting insight into the way Newman viewed the relationship between faith and learning is offered in one of these lectures:

> Knowledge is one thing, virtue is another; good sense is not conscience, refinement is not humility, nor is largeness and justness of view faith. Philosophy, however enlightened, however profound, gives no command over the passions, no influential motives, no vivifying principles. Liberal education makes not the Christian, not the Catholic, but the gentleman. It is well to be a gentleman, it is well to have a cultivated intellect, a delicate taste, a candid, equitable, dispassionate mind, a noble and courteous bearing in the conduct of life—these are the connatural qualities of a large knowledge; they are objects of a university; I am advocating, I shall illustrate and insist upon them; but still, I repeat, they are no guarantee for sanctity or even for conscientiousness, they may attach to the man of the world, to the profligate, to the heartless— pleasant, alas, and attractive as he shows when decked out in them. . . . Quarry the granite rock with razors, or moor the vessel with a thread of silk; then may you hope with such keen and delicate instruments as human knowledge and human reason to contend against those giants, the passion and the pride of man. . . .[5]

The Dublin lectures were an enormous success; Newman's only difficulty occurred during his second talk when the audience had some difficulty hearing him because a brass band, sponsored by the St. Vincent de Paul Society, began playing enthusiastically in an adjoining room! The new Catholic university opened in November of 1854 with an impressive faculty and curriculum, but with an initial enrollment of about 20 students. One of Newman's innovations, unusual for the times, was the introduction of evening classes for young working people who were only able to attend college on a part-time basis.

The university comprised several separate residences and tutorial houses in the area surrounding St. Stephen's Green in Dublin where Newman rented a house for himself and a few undergraduates. The rector provided the students with a billiard room, encouraged extracurricular activities such as music, drama and debating, and let the young people keep their own horses.

However, the Irish bishops apparently expected that the university be run more along the lines of a seminary and Archbishop Cullen was soon writing Rome to complain that "the young men are allowed to go out at all hours, to smoke, etc. All this makes it clear that Father Newman does not give enough attention to details."[6]

One of the details Newman did find important was the construction of a university church which, he felt, would be a visible reminder of the university's direction and also be a bond of unity between the various tutorial houses. He hired as his architect a young English artist, also a former Anglican clergyman, John Hungerford Pollen. After his first meeting with Newman, who was then 53, Pollen wrote his fiancee, "I found him most kind, ever so nice, and full of fun."[7]

Newman's university church still stands on the south side of St. Stephen's Green and appears very much today as it did when it first opened in 1856. Newman preached frequently from the church's marble pulpit, but his sermons were not as popular in Ireland as they had been in England. At St. Mary's in Oxford, scarcely 15 years before, students and faculty crowded the aisles to hear him preach; in Dublin, Newman's congregation seems to have consisted mainly of senior citizens. "If I preached regularly," he wrote a friend, "I should have a large congregation of lawyers and old ladies."[8] He was also amused to discover, when checking the financial records, that the collection doubled on those Sundays when he preached.

Eight of Newman's Irish university homilies are printed in the first section of his book, *Sermons Preached on Various Occasions* and they remain, over a century later, a wonderful statement on the relationship between higher learning and religious faith. Newman never saw a conflict between the two, rather, he desired a much greater integration between "secular" studies and theological learning:

> Here, then, I conceive, is the object of the Holy See and the Catholic Church in setting up Universities; it is to reunite things which were in the beginning joined together by God, and have been put asunder by man. . . . I wish the intellect to range with the utmost freedom, and religion to enjoy an equal freedom; but what I am stipulating for is that they should be found in one and the same place, and exemplified in the same persons. I want to destroy that diversity of centres, which puts everything into confusion by creating a contrariety of influences. I wish the same spots and the same individuals to be at once oracles of philosophy and shrines of devotion. It will not satisfy me, what satisfies so many, to have two independent systems, intellectual and religious, going at once side by side, by a sort of division of labour, and only acciden-

tally brought together. It will not satisfy me,
if religion is here, and science there, and young
men converse with science all day, and lodge
with religion in the evening. It is not touching
the evil, to which these remarks have been
directed, if young men eat and drink and sleep
in one place, and think in another: I want the
same roof to contain both the intellectual and
moral discipline. Devotion is not a sort of
finish given to the sciences; nor is science a sort
of feather in the cap, if I may so express myself, an ornament and set-off to devotion. I
want the intellectual layman to be religious,
and the devout ecclesiastic to be intellectual.[9]

The Catholic University project eventually ended
a failure. Middle-class Irish Catholics were unable to
appreciate the value of higher education except for
professional training, and English Catholics were unwilling to send their sons off to Ireland for college. From
the beginning the university was plagued with serious
financial problems, but the greatest obstacle to Newman's success came from the Irish hierarchy. The
bishops saw the need for a Catholic university, but
they had a provincial view of higher education, were
unwilling to involve the laity in the university's financial
management and by their inability to give decisive
direction when it was needed, undermined many of
Newman's best efforts. Newman returned to England
in 1858 and his resignation as rector was accepted by
the bishops a year later. "He shed cheerfulness as a
sunbeam sheds light," said John Hungerford Pollen of
Newman's days in Ireland, "even while many difficulties
were pressing."[10]

After his return, Newman spent the next few
years at Birmingham in comparative retirement, coping
with the problems of a school for boys run by the

Oratorians. These days, as he approached his 60th birthday, were probably the worst in his life—a time when Newman felt very useless and very much a failure.

Then Charles Kingsley's sudden attack in *Macmillan's Magazine* set the stage for Newman to compose his autobiography, the *Apologia Pro Vita Sua.* This book was published in 1864 and public opinion, both within and without the church, began to change in Newman's favor. The struggles were not over, but his life had turned a corner.

Vatican Council I, in 1870, brought into sharp focus tensions that had always existed between Newman and certain members of the English Catholic community. Newman's basic attitude towards life was open and expansive. He once told a group of scientists:

> I for my part wish to stand on good terms with all kinds of knowledge, and have no intention of quarrelling with any, and would open my heart, if not my intellect, . . . to the whole circle of truth, and would tender at least a recognition and hospitality even to those studies which are strangers to me, and would speed them on their way. . . .[11]

However, some of Newman's coreligionists, especially those who were converts to Catholicism, took a less accepting view. They saw their new religion primarily as a bulwark against modern scientific and political thought, particularly Darwinism and liberalism, which was gaining wide acceptance in the 19th century. These movements, the converts feared, would mean the end, not only of traditional values, but of organized religion as well. This conservative faction among the English Catholic community is known to history as the

"Ultramontane" party. Its adherents, threatened by
the inroads of modern thought, tended to overemphasize
the dogmatic aspects of Catholicism symbolized by
papal authority which resided "beyond the mountain,"
in Rome. At the time of Vatican Council I, the Ultramontane viewpoint dominated the English Catholic press
and its adherents mounted a frenzied campaign which
almost seemed to turn the pope into an oracle indepen-
dent of the church.

Newman walked a different road; his whole aim
in writing *An Essay on the Development of Christian
Doctrine,* for example, had been to show how religious
truth and Christian values had been preserved throughout the centuries despite differing historical situations
and conflicting ideologies. Newman had become a
Catholic because he was convinced that the center of
historical Christianity, whether in the 5th, the 16th or
the 19th centuries, was St. Peter's successor, the Bishop
of Rome. He believed, further, in the infallibility of
the church; that the Lord was with the Christian community to protect it from error seemed, to Newman,
to be a necessary inference from the church's role as
teacher and guardian of revelation:

> Go through the long annals of church history,
> century after century, and say, was there ever
> a time when her bishops, and notably the
> Bishop of Rome, were slow to give their testi-
> mony on behalf of the moral and revealed
> law and to suffer for their obedience to it?
> Ever a time when they forgot that they had a
> message to deliver to the world—not the task
> merely of administering spiritual consolation,
> or of making the sickbed easy, or of training
> up good members of society, or of "serving
> tables" . . . but specially and directly, a def-

inite message to high and low, from the
world's maker, whether men would hear or
whether they would forbear?[12]

Newman had noticed, especially in his study of the
early church, that popes had always seemed to act, in
disputed matters of faith, as if they had the right to the
last word, as if they, too, shared in Christ's guarantee
to his church that the Holy Spirit would protect it from
error and guide it to all truth. So Newman accepted
the infallibility of the pope—that the Bishop of Rome
as head of the church, under very special circumstances, was protected from officially teaching religious
error. But Newman was very careful not to exaggerate
the place of this extraordinary charism in the life of
the church:

> A Pope is not *inspired;* he has no inherent
> gift of divine knowledge, but when he speaks
> *ex cathedra,* he may say little or much, but
> he is simply protected from saying what is
> untrue. I know you will find flatterers and
> partizani such as those whom St. Francis de
> Sales calls "the Pope's lackies," who say much
> more than this, but they may enjoy their own
> opinion, they cannot bind the faith of
> Catholics.[13]

When Vatican Council I officially defined papal
infallibility in 1870, its understanding of the pope's
role in the church was remarkably similar to Newman's
own moderate view and very different from the theological extravagances of the Ultramontane party.

Despite his many disappointments, Newman never
lost faith in the church, never once regretted the
decision he had made the day he entered the Catholic
community so many years before. "(I) testify my simple

loving adhesion to the Catholic Roman Church," he wrote late in life, "and did I wish to give a reason for this full and absolute devotion, what should, what can I say but that those great and burning truths which I learned when a boy from evangelical teachings, I have found impressed on my heart with fresh and ever-increasing force by the Holy Roman Church."[14]

By the late 1870's, Newman's long life seemed to be drawing to an uneventful close. Many years earlier, soon after his conversion, he had written a friend, Maria Giberne, "We are called into God's Church for something; not for nothing surely. Let us wait and be cheerful, and be sure that good is destined for us, and that we are too made useful."[15] But a sense of usefulness as a Catholic proved elusive. In the last pages of his private journal, Newman reveals his feelings of failure and wonderment over the injustices he had suffered from certain individuals within the church.

The final chapter of his long life was written in a way he never expected. The suspicions and misunderstandings which had haunted him for over 30 years suddenly dissolved. A brief, final entry in his diary explains why: "Since writing the above, I have been made a Cardinal."[16]

A new pope in Rome, and a gradual realization within the Catholic community of Newman's enormous gifts and great love of his church, had caused him to be named a cardinal by Leo XIII in 1879. He accepted the honor, not because it was a high ecclesiastical office, but for what it represented. "The cloud is lifted from me forever," he told his community at Birmingham; the journey begun so many years before at Oxford was nearing its completion.

Newman was called into God's church for some-

thing. Seventy years after his death in 1890 there would
be another Vatican Council. The neglected realities
of the faith which he had labored so long to reawaken
within the church—religious liberty, a sense of the
church in the modern world, fidelity to conscience, the
role of the laity and a return to the sources of scripture—
would receive at this Second Vatican Council the
emphasis and attention they deserved.

Some consider his sermon "Ventures of Faith"
the finest homily Newman ever preached from the pulpit
of St. Mary's. He described the way Jesus once asked
James and John if they could venture for him, if they
could drink the cup that he would drink. "We are able,"
the young followers of the Lord had replied enthusiastically, without really knowing the consequences.
Newman observed that these words, "we are able,"
touch the heart of what it means to follow Jesus, the
fullest meaning of Christian faith—to make a *venture*
for eternal life; to risk present happiness for the sake
of a future promise.

People said of Newman at Oxford that he didn't
want to get on in the world; the prizes other men
valued—prestige, power or preferment—were not the
treasures of Newman's heart. He had heard the Lord's
call; he had answered, "I am able," and Newman's life
became not only a momentous quest for truth, but a
moment by moment *venture*—a risking, in faith, of all
he had for the sake of a future promise. He drank the
cup of the Lord, experienced bitter days in all of life's
seasons and then, in the deep winter of his journey,
was suddenly surprised to discover that flowers had
appeared in his land. It was the coming in of a second
spring:

We have familiar experience of the order, the constancy, the perpetual renovation of the material world which surrounds us. Frail and transitory as is every part of it, restless and migratory as are its elements, never-ceasing as are its changes, still it abides. It is bound together by a law of permanence, it is set up in unity; and, though it is ever dying, it is ever coming to life again. Dissolution does but give birth to fresh modes of organization, and one death is the parent of a thousand lives. Each hour, as it comes, is but a testimony, how fleeting, yet how secure, how certain, is the great whole. It is like an image on the waters, which is ever the same, though the waters ever flow. Change upon change— yet one change cries out to another, like the alternate Seraphim, in praise and in glory of their Maker. The sun sinks to rise again; the day is swallowed up in the gloom of the night, to be born out of it, as fresh as if it had never been quenched. Spring passes into summer, and through summer and autumn into winter, only the more surely, by its own ultimate return, to triumph over that grave, toward which it resolutely hastened from its first hour. We mourn over the blossoms of May, because they are to wither; but we know, withal, that May is one day to have its revenge upon November, by the revolution of that solemn circle which never stops—which teaches us in our height of hope, ever to be sober, and in our depth of desolation, never to despair.[17]

Footnotes

Chapter 1

Venture of Faith

1. C. S. Dessain, "The Importance of Newman," in *Spode House Review: Occasional Papers 3* (Rugeley-Staffs: Spode House, 1976), pp. 6-16.
2. John Henry Newman, *Apologia Pro Vita Sua* (1864: rpt. New York: Norton, 1968), p. 16.
3. Ibid., p. 16.
4. Cited in Valentine Fletcher and Humphrey Crookenden, *Newman's Oxford* (Oxford: Oxonian Press Ltd., 1966), p. 8.
5. *Apologia Pro Vita Sua, op. cit.,* p. 96.
6. Cited in C. S. Dessain, *Newman's Spiritual Themes* (Dublin: Veritas Publications, 1977), p. 21.
7. Cited in Louis Bouyer, *Newman: His Life and Spirituality* (New York: Meridian Books, Inc., 1960), p. 235.
8. Ibid., p. 237.
9. Ibid., pp. 241-242.
10. *Poems of Gerard Manly Hopkins* (Mt. Vernon: Peter Pauper Press), p. 36. Printed by permission of Oxford University Press.

Chapter 2

Emotion, and Faith

1. Meriol Trevor, *Newman, The Pillar of the Cloud* (Garden City: Doubleday & Company, Inc., 1962), pp. 277-278.

2. John Henry Newman, "The Gospel Sign Addressed to Faith," *Parochial and Plain Sermons* (London: Longmans & Co., 1891), VI, pp. 108-109.

3. Ibid., pp. 109-110.

4. John Henry Newman, "The Religious Use of Excited Feelings," *Parochial and Plain Sermons* (London: Longmans & Co., 1894), I, p. 118.

5. Cited by Louis Bouyer, *Newman: His Life and Spirituality* (New York: Meridian Books, Inc., 1960), p. 237.

6. John Henry Newman, "The Ventures of Faith," *Parochial and Plain Sermons* (London: Longmans & Co., 1900), IV, p. 299.

7. Op. cit., I, pp. 122-123.

Chapter 3

Heart Speaks to Heart

1. Cited in Valentine Fletcher and Humphrey Crookenden, *Newman's Oxford* (Oxford: Oxonian Press Ltd., 1966), p. 8.

2. John Henry Newman, "Personal Influence, The Means of Propagating the Truth," *Fifteen Sermons Preached Before the University of Oxford* (1871: rpt. London: S.P.C.K., 1970), p. 95.

4. Ibid., p. 89.

5. Ibid., p. 90.

6. Ibid., p. 76.

7. Ibid., pp. 93-94.

8. Ibid., p. 94.

9. Ibid., p. 92.

10. Ibid., pp. 96-97.

11. Ibid., pp. 96-97.

12. Cited in Meriol Trevor, *Newman, the Pillar of the Cloud* (Garden City: Doubleday and Company, Inc., 1962), p. 252.

13. Ibid., p. 358.

14. Urban Young, C. P., "Newman and Dominic," *Newman and Littlemore,* (Littlemore: The Salesian Fathers, 1945), p. 31.

Chapter 4

Christ Upon the Waters

1. John Henry Newman, "The Second Spring," *Sermons Preached on Various Occasions* (London: Longmans, Green and Co., 1898), p. 171.

2. Ibid., p. 172.

3. John Henry Newman, "Christ Upon the Waters," *Sermons Preached on Various Occasions,* op. cit., p. 135.

4. *Sayings of Cardinal Newman* (Blackrock, Ireland: Carraig Books, 1976), p. 5.

5. *Sermons Preached on Various Occasions,* op. cit., p. 325.

6. "Christ Upon the Waters," op. cit., p. 143.

7. Ibid., p. 144.

8. Ibid., p. 149.

9. Ibid., p. 154.

10. John Henry Newman, *Historical Sketches,* Vol. II (London: Longmans, Green and Co., 1920), p. 1.

11. "Christ Upon the Waters," op. cit., pp. 123, 124.

Chapter 5

Divine Calls

1. John Henry Newman, *Apologia Pro Vita Sua* (1894: rpt. New York: Norton, 1968), p. 184.

2. John Henry Newman, "Divine Calls," *Parochial and Plain Sermons* (London: Longmans, Green and Co., 1896), VIII, p. 29.

3. *Apologia,* op. cit., p. 24.

4. *Parochial and Plain Sermons,* VIII, op. cit., p. 28.

5. Ibid., pp. 28-29.

6. Ibid., pp. 29-30.

7. John Henry Newman, "Ventures of Faith," *Parochial and Plain Sermons* (London: Longmans, Green and Co., 1900), IV, p. 304.

8. Ibid., pp. 304-305.

9. *Parochial and Plain Sermons,* VIII, op. cit., pp. 23-24.

10. Ibid., p. 24.

11. John Henry Newman, *Apologia Pro Vita Sua* (1864: rpt. New York: Norton, 1968), p. 98.

12. Ibid., p. 99.

13. *Parochial and Plain Sermons,* VIII, op. cit., p. 32.

Chapter 6

The Kindly Light

1. Meriol Trevor, *Newman, Light in Winter* (Garden City: Doubleday and Company, Inc., 1963), p. 266.

2. "Sect Manual for Army Chaplains," *Time,* July 3, 1978, p. 76.

3. Meriol Trevor, *Newman, The Pillar of the Cloud* (Garden City: Doubleday and Company, Inc., 1962), p. 348.

4. John Henry Newman, "Truth Hidden When Not Sought After," *Parochial and Plain Sermons* (London: Longmans, Green and Co., 1896), VIII, p. 188.

5. Ibid., pp. 190-191.

6. John Henry Newman, "Dispositions for Faith," *Sermons Preached on Various Occasions* (London: Longmans, Green and Co., 1898), p. 65.

7. John Henry Newman, "The Allegiance of Catholics and the Primacy of Conscience," from *The Difficulties of Anglicans,* Vol. II, in *A Newman Reader,* ed. Francis X. Connolly (Garden City: Doubleday Image, 1964), pp. 381-382.

8. Ibid., p. 383.

9. Newman, "Truth Hidden When Not Sought After," op. cit., p. 195.

10. John Henry Newman, *Callista: A Sketch of the Third Century* (New York, P. J. Kenedy & Sons, n.d.), p. 247.

11. John Henry Newman, *An Essay in Aid of a Grammar of Assent* (Garden City: Doubleday Image, 1955), p. 101.

12. Louis Bouyer, *Newman: His Life and Spirituality* (New York: Meridian Books, Inc., 1960), pp. 143-144.

Chapter 7

Discipleship and Disappointments

1. Cited in John Henry Newman, *Apologia Pro Vita Sua* (1864; rpt. New York: Norton, 1968), p. 373.

2. Meriol Trevor, *Newman, Light in Winter* (Garden City: Doubleday and Company, Inc., 1963), p. 334.

3. Susan Chitty, *The Beast and the Monk* (New York: Mason Charter, 1975), p. 231.

4. Vincent Ferrer Blehl, S. J., ed., *Cardinal Newman's Best Plain Sermons* (New York: Herder and Herder, 1964), p. vii.

5. Cited by Louis Bouyer, *Newman: His Life and Spirituality* (New York: Meridian Books, Inc., 1960), p. 355.

6. John Henry Newman, "Jeremiah, A Lesson for the Disappointed," *Parochial and Plain Sermons* (London: Longmans, Green and Company, 1896), VIII, pp. 129-130.

7. Ibid., p. 138.

8. Trevor, op. cit., p. 47.

9. Bouyer, op. cit., p. 266.

10. John Henry Newman, "Affliction, A School of Comfort," *Parochial and Plain Sermons* (London: Longmans, Green and Company, 1896), V, pp. 308-309.

11. Ibid., pp. 307-308.

Chapter 8

The Second Spring

1. Cited by Louis Bouyer, *Newman: His Life and Spirituality* (New York: Meridian Books, Inc. 1960), pp. 253-254.

2. Ibid., p. 355.

3. Meriol Trevor, *Newman, The Pillar of the Cloud* (Garden City: Doubleday and Company, Inc., 1962), p. 458.

4. Meriol Trevor, *Newman's Journey* (Glasgow: Collins, Fontana Library, 1974), p. 139.

5. John Henry Newman, "Knowledge Its Own End," *The Idea of a University* (London: Longmans, Green and Company, 1899), pp. 120-121.

6. Meriol Trevor, *Newman, Light in Winter* (Garden City: Doubleday and Company, Inc., 1963), p. 49.

7. Ibid., p. 60.

8. Ibid., p. 158.

9. John Henry Newman, "Intellect, The Instrument of Religious Training," *Sermons Preached on Various Occasions* (London: Longmans, Green and Company, 1898), pp. 12-13.

10. Meriol Trevor, *Newman, Light in Winter,* op. cit., p. 61.

11. John Henry Newman, "Christianity and Scientific Investigation," *The Idea of a University,* op. cit., p. 456.

12. John Henry Newman, *Certain Difficulties Felt by Anglicans in Catholic Teaching* (London: Longmans, Green and Company, 1819), II, p. 197.

13. Charles Stephen Dessain, ed., *The Letters and Diaries of John Henry Newman* (London: Thomas Nelson and Sons Ltd., 1961), XXV, p. 299.

14. Cited by Charles Stephen Dessain, "Newman as an Anglican and as a Catholic," in *Spode House Review: Occasional Papers 3* (Rugeley-Staffs: Spode House, 1976), pp. 36-37.

15. Charles Stephen Dessain, ed., *The Letters and Diaries of John Henry Newman* (London: Thomas Nelson and Sons Ltd., 1961), XI, p. 96.

16. Bouyer, op. cit., p. 384.

17. John Henry Newman, "The Second Spring," *Sermons Preached on Various Occasions,* op. cit., pp. 163-164.